WORDPERFECT® 6.1
for Windows™
SIMPLIFIED

IDG's

Series

by: maranGraphics' Development Group

IDG BOOKS

IDG Books Worldwide, Inc.
An International Data Group Company

Foster City, California ✦ Indianapolis, Indiana ✦ Boston, Massachusetts

WordPerfect® 6.1 for Windows™ Simplified

Published by
IDG Books Worldwide, Inc.
An International Data Group Company
919 E. Hillsdale Blvd., Suite 400
Foster City, CA 94404
(415) 655-3000

Copyright© 1994 by maranGraphics Inc.
5755 Coopers Avenue
Mississauga, Ontario, Canada
L4Z 1R9

WordPerfect 6.1 for Windows
screen shots, © 1991, 1994
Novell, Inc. All Rights Reserved.
Used with permission.

Library of Congress Catalog Card No.: 94-079407

ISBN: 1-56884-665-7

Printed in the United States of America

10 9 8 7 6

Distributed in the United States by IDG Books Worldwide, Inc.

Distributed by Computer and Technical Books in Miami, Florida, for South America and the Caribbean; by Longman Singapore in Singapore, Malaysia, Thailand, and Korea; by Toppan Co. Ltd. in Japan; by IDG Communications HK in Hong Kong; by WoodsLane Pty. Ltd. in Australia and New Zealand; and by Transworld Publishers Ltd. in the U.K. and Europe.

For general information on IDG Books in the U.S., including information on discounts and premiums, contact IDG Books at 800-762-2974 or 317-895-5200.

For U.S. Corporate Sales and quantity discounts, contact maranGraphics at 800-469-6616, ext. 206.

For information on international sales of IDG Books, contact Helen Saraceni at 415-655-3021, Fax number 415-655-3295.

For information on translations, contact Marc Jeffrey Mikulich, Director of Rights and Licensing, at IDG Books Worldwide. Fax Number 415-655-3295.

For sales inquiries and special prices for bulk quantities, write to the address above or call IDG Books Worldwide at 415-655-3000.

For information on using IDG Books in the classroom, or ordering examination copies, contact Jim Kelly at 800-434-2086.

Trademark Acknowledgments

maranGraphics Inc. has attempted to include trademark information for products, services and companies referred to in this guide. Although maranGraphics Inc. has made reasonable efforts in gathering this information, it cannot guarantee its accuracy.

WordPerfect and Grammatik are registered trademarks of Novell, Inc. within the United States and other countries.

Microsoft, MS-DOS and Microsoft Mouse are registered trademarks and Windows is a trademark of Microsoft Corporation.

©1994
maranGraphics, Inc.

The animated characters are the copyright of maranGraphics, Inc.

U.S. Corporate Sales	**U.S. Trade Sales**
Contact maranGraphics at (800) 469-6616, ext. 206 or Fax (905) 890-9434.	Contact IDG Books at (800) 434-3422 or (415) 655-3000.

About IDG Books Worldwide

Welcome to the world of IDG Books Worldwide.

IDG Books Worldwide, Inc., is a subsidiary of International Data Group, the world's largest publisher of business and computer-related information and the leading global provider of information services on information technology. IDG was founded more than 25 years ago and now employs more than 5,700 people worldwide. IDG publishes more than 200 computer publications in 63 countries (see listing below). Forty million people read one or more IDG publications each month.

Launched in 1990, IDG Books is today the fastest-growing publisher of computer and business books in the United States. We are proud to have received 3 awards from the Computer Press Association in recognition of editorial excellence, and our best-selling ...For Dummies series has more than 10 million copies in print with translations in more than 20 languages. IDG Books, through a recent joint venture with IDG's Hi-Tech Beijing, became the first U.S. publisher to publish a computer book in the People's Republic of China. In record time, IDG Books has become the first choice for millions of readers around the world who want to learn how to better manage their businesses.

Our mission is simple: Every IDG book is designed to bring extra value and skill-building instructions to the reader. Our books are written by experts who understand and care about our readers. The knowledge base of our editorial staff comes from years of experience in publishing, education, and journalism — experience which we use to produce books for the '90s. In short, we care about books, so we attract the best people. We devote special attention to details such as audience, interior design, use of icons, and illustrations. And because we use an efficient process of authoring, editing, and desktop publishing our books electronically, we can spend more time ensuring superior content and spend less time on the technicalities of making books.

You can count on our commitment to deliver high-quality books at competitive prices on topics customers want to read about. At IDG, we value quality, and we have been delivering quality for more than 25 years. You'll find no better book on a subject than an IDG book.

John Kilcullen
President and CEO
IDG Books Worldwide, Inc.

IDG Books Worldwide, Inc., is a subsidiary of International Data Group. The officers are Patrick J. McGovern, Founder and Board Chairman; Walter Boyd, President. International Data Group's publications include: ARGENTINA'S Computerworld Argentina, Infoworld Argentina; AUSTRALIA'S Computerworld Australia, Australian PC World, Australian Macworld, Network World, Mobile Business Australia, Reseller, IDG Sources; AUSTRIA'S Computerwelt Oesterreich, PC Test; BRAZIL'S Computerworld, Gamepro, Game Power, Mundo IBM, Mundo Unix, PC World, Super Game; BELGIUM'S Data News (CW) BULGARIA'S Computerworld Bulgaria, Ediworld, PC & Mac World Bulgaria, Network World Bulgaria; CANADA'S CIO Canada, Computerworld Canada, Graduate Computerworld, InfoCanada, Network World Canada; CHILE'S Computerworld Chile, Informatica; COLOMBIA'S Computerworld Colombia, PC World; CZECH REPUBLIC'S Computerworld, Elektronika, PC World; DENMARK'S Communications World, Computerworld Danmark, Macintosh Produktkatalog, Macworld Danmark, PC World Danmark, PC World Produktguide, Tech World, Windows World; ECUADOR'S PC World Ecuador; EGYPT'S Computerworld (CW) Middle East, PC World Middle East; FINLAND'S MikroPC, Tietoviikko, Tietoverkko; FRANCE'S Distributique, GOLDEN MAC, PC World, Languages & Systems, Le Guide du Monde Informatique, Le Monde Informatique, Telecoms & Reseaux; GERMANY'S Computerwoche, Computerwoche Focus, Computerwoche Extra, Computerwoche Karriere, Information Management, Macwelt, Netzwelt, PC Welt, PC Woche, Publish, Unit; GREECE'S Infoworld, PC Games; HUNGARY'S Computerworld SZT, PC World; HONG KONG'S Computerworld Hong Kong, PC World Hong Kong; INDIA'S Computers & Communications; IRELAND'S ComputerScope; ISRAEL'S Computerworld Israel, PC World Israel; ITALY'S Computerworld Italia, Lotus Magazine, Macworld Italia, Networking Italia, PC Shopping, PC World Italia; JAPAN'S Computerworld Today, Information Systems World, Macworld Japan, Nikkei Personal Computing, SunWorld Japan, Windows World; KENYA'S East African Computer News; KOREA'S Computerworld Korea, Macworld Korea, PC World Korea; MEXICO'S Compu Edicion, Compu Manufactura, Computacion/Punto de Venta, Computerworld Mexico, MacWorld, Mundo Unix, PC World, Windows; THE NETHERLANDS' Computer! Totaal, Computable (CW), LAN Magazine, MacWorld, Totaal "Windows"; NEW ZEALAND'S Computer Listings, Computerworld New Zealand, New Zealand PC World, Network World; NIGERIA'S PC World Africa; NORWAY'S Computerworld Norge, C/World, Lotusworld Norge, Macworld Norge, Networld, PC World Ekspress, PC World Norge, PC World's Produktguide, Publish& Multimedia World, Student Data, Unix World, Windowsworld; IDG Direct Response; PAKISTAN'S PC World Pakistan; PANAMA'S PC World Panama; PERU'S Computerworld Peru, PC World; PEOPLE'S REPUBLIC OF CHINA'S China Computerworld, China Infoworld, Electronics Today/Multimedia World, Electronics International, Electronic Product World, China Network World, PC and Communications Magazine, PC World China, Software World Magazine, Telecom Product World; IDG HIGH TECH BEIJING'S New Product World; IDG SHENZHEN'S Computer News Digest; PHILIPPINES' Computerworld Philippines, PC Digest (PCW); POLAND'S Computerworld Poland, PC World/Komputer; PORTUGAL'S Cerebro/PC World, Correio Informatico/Computerworld, Informatica & Comunicacoes Catalogo, MacIn, Nacional de Produtos; ROMANIA'S Computerworld, PC World; RUSSIA'S Computerworld-Moscow, Mir - PC, Sety; SINGAPORE'S Computerworld Southeast Asia, PC World Singapore; SLOVENIA'S Monitor Magazine; SOUTH AFRICA'S Computer Mail (CIO),Computing S.A.,Network World S.A., Software World; SPAIN'S Advanced Systems, Amiga World, Computerworld Espana, Communicaciones World, Macworld Espana, NeXTWORLD, Super Juegos Magazine (GamePro), PC World Espana, Publish; SWEDEN'S Attack, ComputerSweden, Corporate Computing, Natverk & Kommunikation, Macworld, Mikrodatorn, PC World, Publishing & Design (CAP), Datalngenjoren, Maxi Data,Windows World; SWITZERLAND'S Computerworld Schweiz, Macworld Schweiz, PC Tip; TAIWAN'S Computerworld Taiwan, PC World Taiwan; THAILAND'S Thai Computerworld; TURKEY'S Computerworld Monitor, Macworld Turkiye, PC World Turkiye; UKRAINE'S Computerworld; UNITED KINGDOM'S Computing /Computerworld, Connexion/Network World, Lotus Magazine, Macworld, Open Computing/Sunworld; UNITED STATES' Advanced Systems, AmigaWorld, Cable in the Classroom, CD Review, CIO, Computerworld, Digital Video, DOS Resource Guide, Electronic Entertainment Magazine, Federal Computer Week, Federal Integrator, GamePro, IDG Books, Infoworld, Infoworld Direct, Laser Event, Macworld, Multimedia World, Network World, PC Letter, PC World, PlayRight, Power PC World, Publish, SWATPro, Video Event; VENEZUELA'S Computerworld Venezuela, PC World; VIETNAM'S PC World Vietnam

Credits

Author and Architect:
Ruth Maran

Copy Developer:
Kelleigh Wing

Technical Consultant:
Wendi Blouin Ewbank

Layout Artist:
Carol Walthers

Illustrators:
Dave de Haas
Dave Ross

Illustration Revisor:
Suzanna Pereira

Screen Artist:
Christie Van Duin

Editors:
Lisa Dickie
Judy Maran
Kelleigh Wing

Post Production:
David McKenna
Kris Gurn
Robert Maran

Acknowledgments

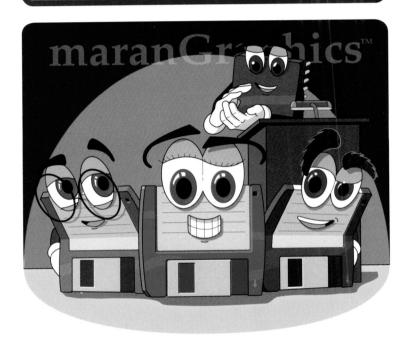

Special thanks to Wendi B. Ewbank for her insight and dedication in ensuring the technical accuracy of this book.

Thanks to Saverio C. Tropiano for his assistance and expert advice.

Thanks to the dedicated staff of maranGraphics, including David de Haas, Lisa Dickie, Judy Maran, Maxine Maran, Robert Maran, Sherry Maran, Suzanna Pereira, Tamara Poliquin, Dave Ross, Christie Van Duin, Carol Walthers and Kelleigh Wing.

Finally, to Richard Maran who originated the easy-to-use graphic format of this guide. Thank you for your inspiration and guidance.

TABLE OF CONTENTS

INTRODUCTION TO WORDPERFECT

Print Your Documents

Change Your Document Display

Using Multiple Documents

WORKING WITH WORDPERFECT

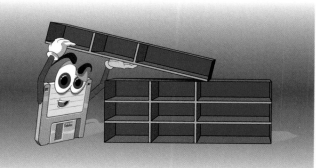

GETTING STARTED

◆ In this chapter you will learn the basic skills needed to use WordPerfect for Windows.

Getting Started	Edit Your Documents	Smart Editing	Save and Open Your Documents	Print Your Documents	Change Your Document Display	Using Multiple Documents

- **Introduction**
- Mouse Basics
- Start WordPerfect
- Enter Text

- Select Commands
- Move Through a Document
- Select Text
- Help

WHAT YOU CAN CREATE WITH WORDPERFECT FOR WINDOWS

PERSONAL AND BUSINESS LETTERS

WordPerfect for Windows helps you produce letters quickly and accurately.

MAILING LISTS

WordPerfect for Windows can merge a document with a list of names and addresses to produce personalized letters.

REPORTS AND MANUALS

WordPerfect for Windows provides editing and formatting features that make it ideal for producing longer documents such as reports and manuals.

MOUSE BASICS

The mouse is a hand-held device that lets you quickly select commands and perform actions.

USING THE MOUSE

◆ Hold the mouse as shown in the diagram. Use your thumb and two rightmost fingers to guide the mouse while your two remaining fingers press the mouse buttons.

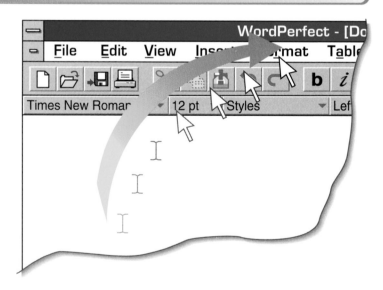

◆ When you move the mouse on your desk, the mouse pointer (I or κ) on your screen moves in the same direction. The mouse pointer changes shape depending on its location on your screen.

PARTS OF THE MOUSE

◆ The mouse has a left and right button. You can use these buttons to:

- open menus
- select commands
- choose options

Note: You will use the left button most of the time.

◆ Under the mouse is a ball that senses movement. To ensure smooth motion of the mouse, you should occasionally remove and clean this ball.

MOUSE TERMS

CLICK

Quickly press and release the left mouse button once.

DOUBLE-CLICK

Quickly press and release the left mouse button twice.

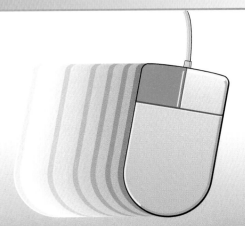

DRAG

When the mouse pointer (▷ or I) is over an object on your screen, press and hold down the left mouse button and then move the mouse.

START WORDPERFECT

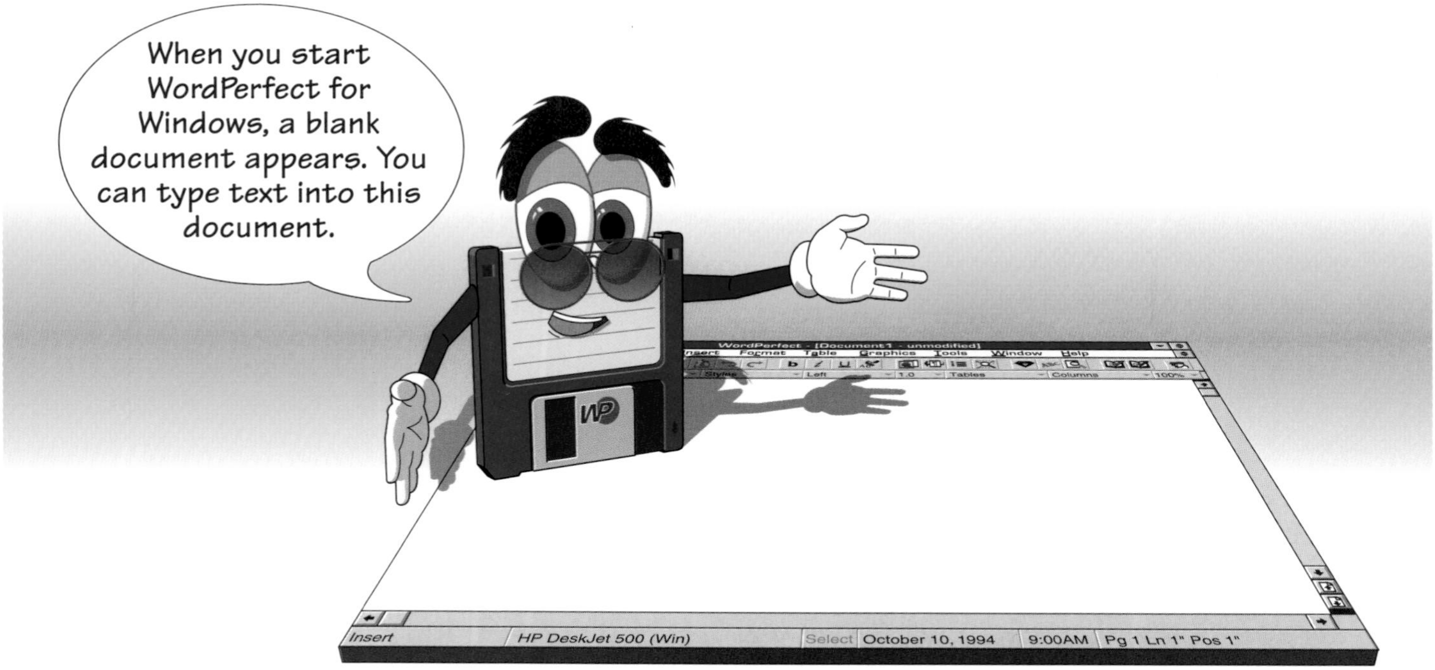
When you start WordPerfect for Windows, a blank document appears. You can type text into this document.
Insert
HP DeskJet 500 (Win)
Select
October 10, 1994
9:00AM
Pg 1 Ln 1" Pos 1"

START WORDPERFECT FOR WINDOWS

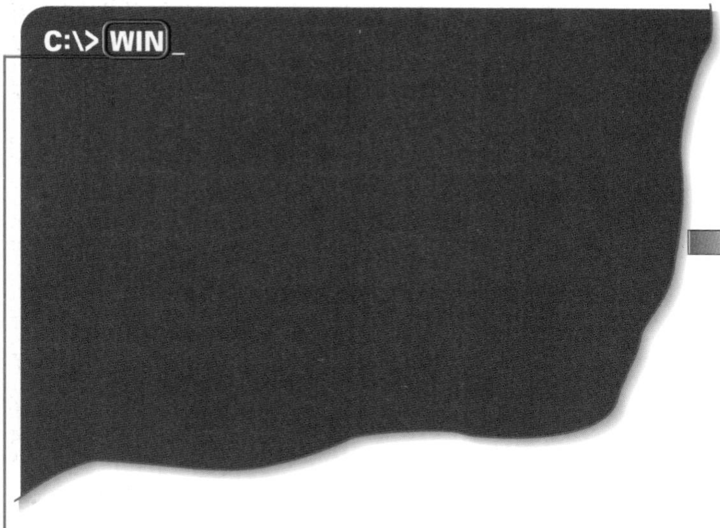
C:\> WIN _

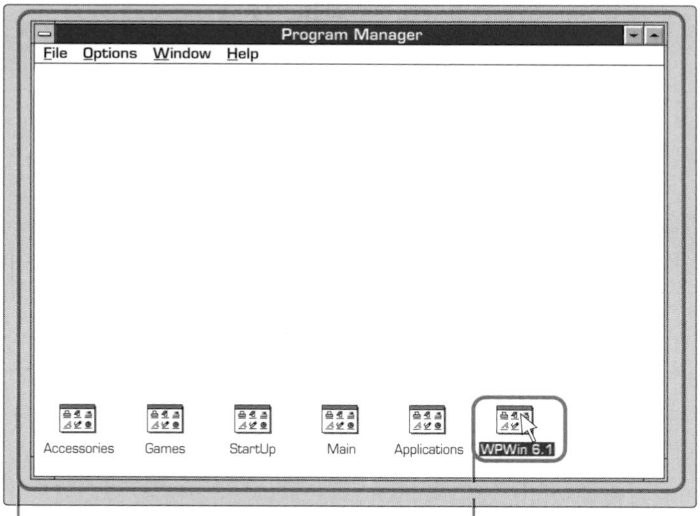
Program Manager
File Options Window Help
Accessories
Games
StartUp
Main
Applications
WPWin 6.1

1 To start WordPerfect for Windows from MS-DOS, type **WIN** and then press Enter.

◆ The **Program Manager** window appears.

2 To open the **WPWin 6.1** group window, move the mouse over this icon and then quickly press the left button twice.

Getting Started	Edit Your Documents	Smart Editing	Save and Open Your Documents	Print Your Documents	Change Your Document Display	Using Multiple Documents

- Introduction
- Mouse Basics
- **Start WordPerfect**
- Enter Text

- Select Commands
- Move Through a Document
- Select Text
- Help

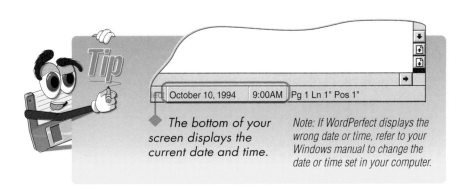

The bottom of your screen displays the current date and time.

Note: If WordPerfect displays the wrong date or time, refer to your Windows manual to change the date or time set in your computer.

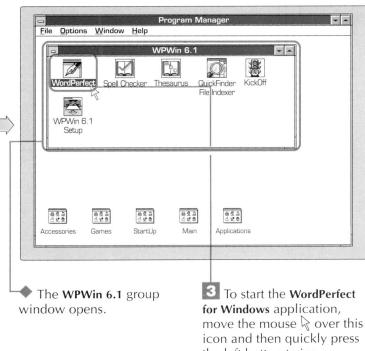

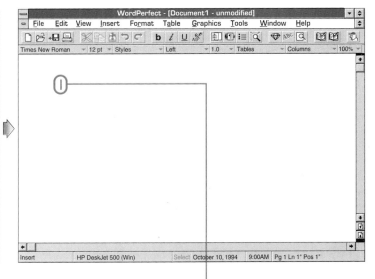

◆ The **WPWin 6.1** group window opens.

3 To start the **WordPerfect for Windows** application, move the mouse over this icon and then quickly press the left button twice.

◆ The **WordPerfect** window appears displaying a blank document.

◆ The flashing line on your screen indicates where the text you type will appear. It is called the **insertion point**.

ENTER TEXT

When typing text in your document, you do not need to press **Enter** at the end of a line. WordPerfect automatically moves the text to the next line. This is called word wrapping.

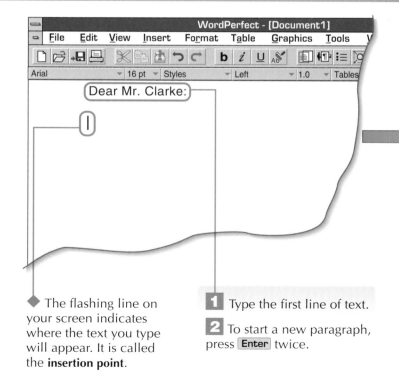

ENTER TEXT

◆ In this book, the design and size of text were changed to make the document easier to read.

Initial or default font	New font
Times New Roman 12 point	**Arial 16 point**

Note: To change the design and size of text, refer to page 104.

◆ To work faster in WordPerfect, display your document in the Draft mode.

Note: To change modes, refer to page 80.

◆ The flashing line on your screen indicates where the text you type will appear. It is called the **insertion point**.

1 Type the first line of text.

2 To start a new paragraph, press **Enter** twice.

Getting Started	Edit Your Documents	Smart Editing	Save and Open Your Documents	Print Your Documents	Change Your Document Display	Using Multiple Documents

- Introduction
- Mouse Basics
- Start WordPerfect
- **Enter Text**

- Select Commands
- Move Through a Document
- Select Text
- Help

When using a typewriter to type a letter, the text au...

When using a word processor to type a letter, the text automatically wraps to the next line as you type.

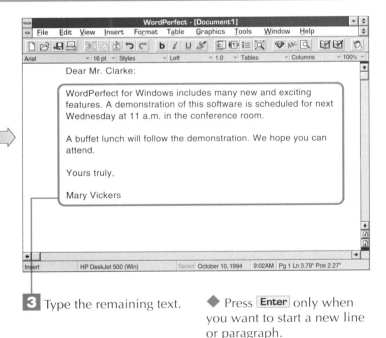

Dear Mr. Clarke:

WordPerfect for Windows includes many new and exciting features. A demonstration of this software is scheduled for next Wednesday at 11 a.m. in the conference room.

A buffet lunch will follow the demonstration. We hope you can attend.

Yours truly,

Mary Vickers

3 Type the remaining text.

◆ Press **Enter** only when you want to start a new line or paragraph.

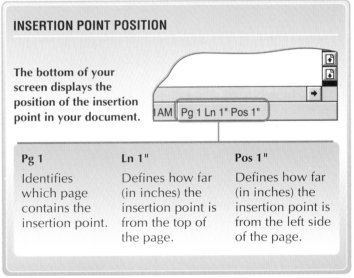

INSERTION POINT POSITION

The bottom of your screen displays the position of the insertion point in your document.

Pg 1	**Ln 1"**	**Pos 1"**
Identifies which page contains the insertion point.	Defines how far (in inches) the insertion point is from the top of the page.	Defines how far (in inches) the insertion point is from the left side of the page.

SELECT COMMANDS

You can open a menu to display a list of related commands. You can then select the command you want to use.

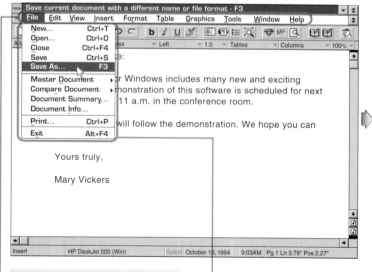

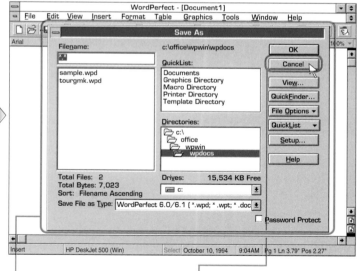

1 To open a menu, move the mouse � over the menu name (example: **File**) and then press the left button.

Note: To close a menu, move the mouse � outside the menu and then press the left button.

2 To select a command, move the mouse � over the command name (example: **Save As**) and then press the left button.

◆ A dialog box appears if WordPerfect requires more information to carry out the command.

3 To close a dialog box, move the mouse � over **Cancel** or **Close** and then press the left button.

Getting Started	Edit Your Documents	Smart Editing	Save and Open Your Documents	Print Your Documents	Change Your Document Display	Using Multiple Documents

- Introduction
- Mouse Basics
- Start WordPerfect
- Enter Text

- **Select Commands**
- Move Through a Document
- Select Text
- Help

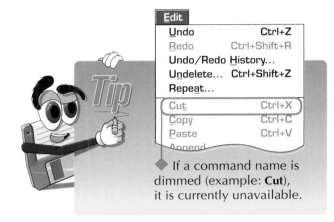

If a command name is dimmed (example: **Cut**), it is currently unavailable.

THE MENUS (USING THE KEYBOARD)

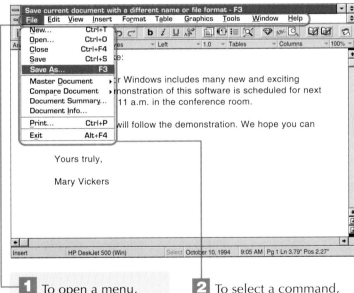

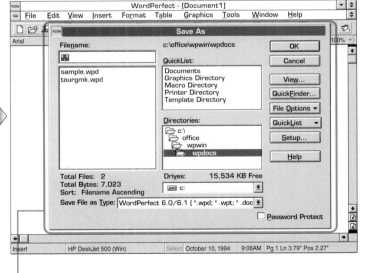

1 To open a menu, press **Alt** followed by the underlined letter in the menu name (example: **F** for **File**).

*Note: To close a menu, press **Alt**.*

2 To select a command, press the underlined letter in the command name (example: **A** for **Save As**).

◆ A dialog box appears if WordPerfect requires more information to carry out the command.

3 To close a dialog box, press **Esc**.

SELECT COMMANDS

You can use the WordPerfect buttons to quickly select the most commonly used commands.

THE WORDPERFECT BUTTONS

Each button displayed on your screen provides a fast method of selecting a menu command.

For example, you can use ⊞ to quickly select the Save command.

File	
New...	Ctrl+T
Open...	Ctrl+O
Close	Ctrl+F4
Save	Ctrl+S
Save As...	F3

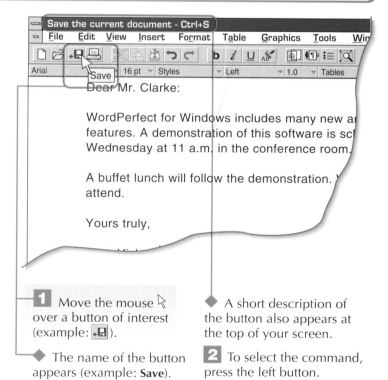

1 Move the mouse over a button of interest (example: ⊞).

◆ The name of the button appears (example: **Save**).

◆ A short description of the button also appears at the top of your screen.

2 To select the command, press the left button.

12

- Introduction
- Mouse Basics
- Start WordPerfect
- Enter Text

- **Select Commands**
- Move Through a Document
- Select Text
- Help

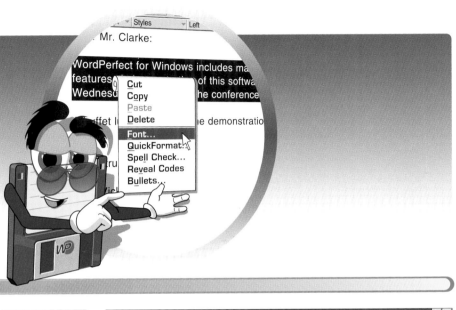

A QuickMenu displays a list of commonly used commands that you can apply to text you select.

THE QUICKMENUS

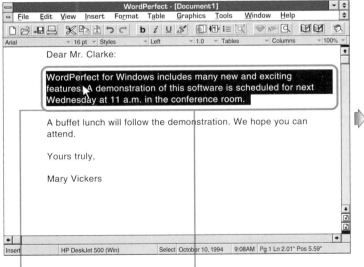

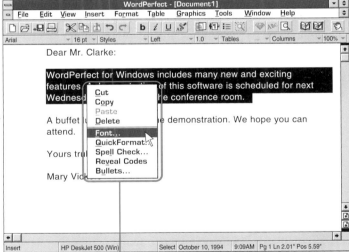

1 Select the text you want to work with.

Note: To select text, refer to page 16.

2 Move the mouse anywhere over the text you selected and then press the **right** button.

◆ A QuickMenu appears.

Note: You can display a QuickMenu over selected text or any other area on your screen.

3 Move the mouse over the command you want to use and then press the left button.

Note: To close the QuickMenu, move the mouse outside the menu and then press the left button.

MOVE THROUGH A DOCUMENT

If you create a long document, your computer screen cannot display all the text at the same time. You must move through the document to view other areas of text.

MOVE TO ANY POSITION ON YOUR SCREEN

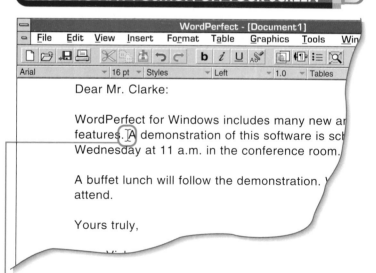

WordPerfect - [Document1]

File   Edit   View   Insert   Format   Table   Graphics   Tools   Win

Arial   16 pt   Styles   Left   1.0   Tables

Dear Mr. Clarke:

WordPerfect for Windows includes many new ar features. A demonstration of this software is sc Wednesday at 11 a.m. in the conference room.

A buffet lunch will follow the demonstration. attend.

Yours truly,

1 To move the insertion point to a different location on your screen, move the mouse I over the location and then press the left button.

VIEW PREVIOUS OR NEXT PAGE

If your document contains more than one page, you can view the previous or next page.

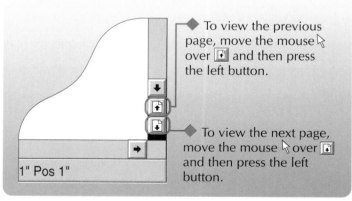

1" Pos 1"

◆ To view the previous page, move the mouse over 🖻 and then press the left button.

◆ To view the next page, move the mouse over 🖻 and then press the left button.

Getting Started	Edit Your Documents	Smart Editing	Save and Open Your Documents	Print Your Documents	Change Your Document Display	Using Multiple Documents

- Introduction
- Mouse Basics
- Start WordPerfect
- Enter Text

- Select Commands
- **Move Through a Document**
- Select Text
- Help

SCROLL UP OR DOWN

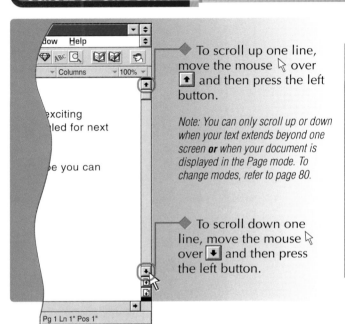

◆ To scroll up one line, move the mouse ↖ over ⬆ and then press the left button.

*Note: You can only scroll up or down when your text extends beyond one screen **or** when your document is displayed in the Page mode. To change modes, refer to page 80.*

◆ To scroll down one line, move the mouse ↖ over ⬇ and then press the left button.

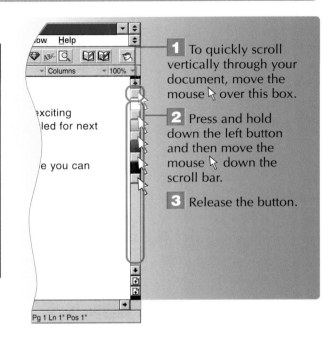

1 To quickly scroll vertically through your document, move the mouse ↖ over this box.

2 Press and hold down the left button and then move the mouse ↖ down the scroll bar.

3 Release the button.

KEYBOARD SHORTCUTS

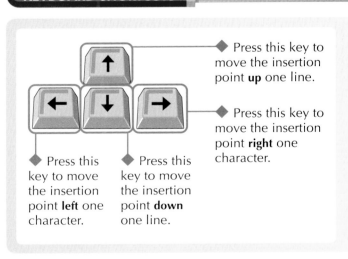

◆ Press this key to move the insertion point **up** one line.

◆ Press this key to move the insertion point **right** one character.

◆ Press this key to move the insertion point **left** one character.

◆ Press this key to move the insertion point **down** one line.

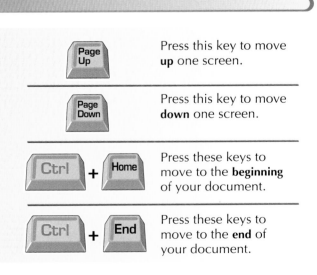

Press this key to move **up** one screen.

Press this key to move **down** one screen.

Press these keys to move to the **beginning** of your document.

Press these keys to move to the **end** of your document.

SELECT TEXT

Before you can use many WordPerfect features, you must first select the text you want to change. Selected text appears highlighted on your screen.

SELECT A WORD

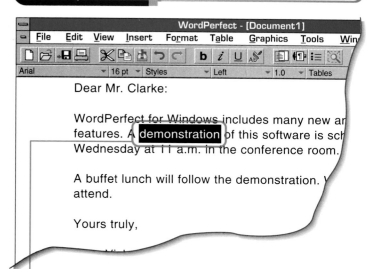

1 Move the mouse I anywhere over the word you want to select and then quickly press the left button twice.

TO CANCEL A TEXT SELECTION

Move the mouse I anywhere outside the selected area and then press the left button.

SELECT A SENTENCE

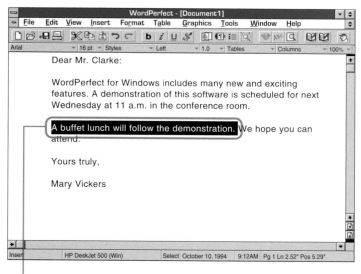

1 Move the mouse I anywhere over the sentence you want to select and then quickly press the left button **three** times.

Getting Started	Edit Your Documents	Smart Editing	Save and Open Your Documents	Print Your Documents	Change Your Document Display	Using Multiple Documents

- Introduction
- Mouse Basics
- Start WordPerfect
- Enter Text

- Select Commands
- Move Through a Document
- **Select Text**
- Help

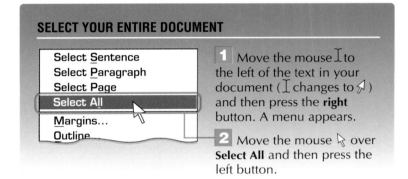

SELECT YOUR ENTIRE DOCUMENT

Select Sentence
Select Paragraph
Select Page
Select All

Margins...
Outline

1 Move the mouse I to the left of the text in your document (I changes to ⬧) and then press the **right** button. A menu appears.

2 Move the mouse ⬧ over **Select All** and then press the left button.

SELECT A PARAGRAPH

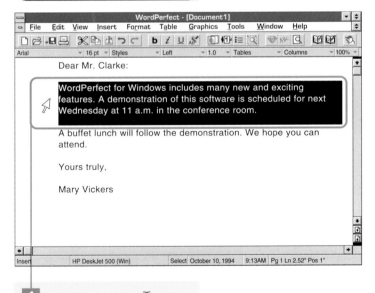

1 Move the mouse I to the left of the paragraph you want to select (I changes to ⬧) and then quickly press the left button twice.

SELECT ANY AMOUNT OF TEXT

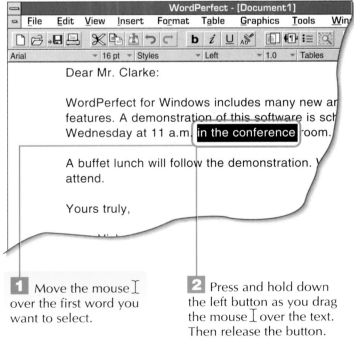

1 Move the mouse I over the first word you want to select.

2 Press and hold down the left button as you drag the mouse I over the text. Then release the button.

HELP

If you forget how to perform a task, you can use the WordPerfect Help feature to obtain information. This can save you time by eliminating the need to refer to other sources.

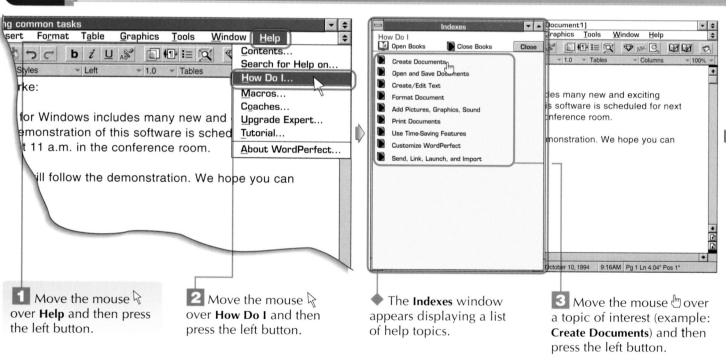

1 Move the mouse ⊾ over **Help** and then press the left button.

2 Move the mouse ⊾ over **How Do I** and then press the left button.

◆ The **Indexes** window appears displaying a list of help topics.

3 Move the mouse ⏥ over a topic of interest (example: **Create Documents**) and then press the left button.

18

Getting Started	Edit Your Documents	Smart Editing	Save and Open Your Documents	Print Your Documents	Change Your Document Display	Using Multiple Documents

- Introduction
- Mouse Basics
- Start WordPerfect
- Enter Text

- Select Commands
- Move Through a Document
- Select Text
- **Help**

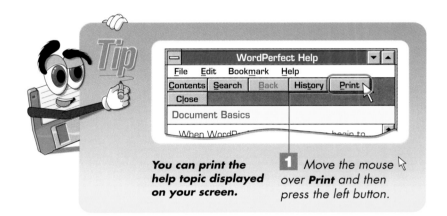

You can print the help topic displayed on your screen.

1 Move the mouse over **Print** and then press the left button.

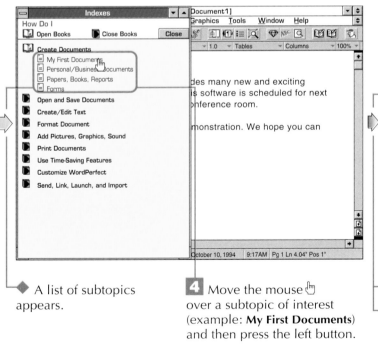

◆ A list of subtopics appears.

4 Move the mouse over a subtopic of interest (example: **My First Documents**) and then press the left button.

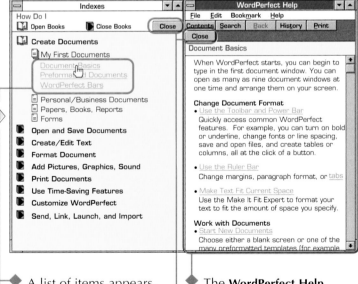

◆ A list of items appears.

5 Move the mouse over an item of interest (example: **Document Basics**) and then press the left button.

◆ The **WordPerfect Help** window appears displaying information on the item you selected.

6 To close a Help window, move the mouse over **Close** and then press the left button.

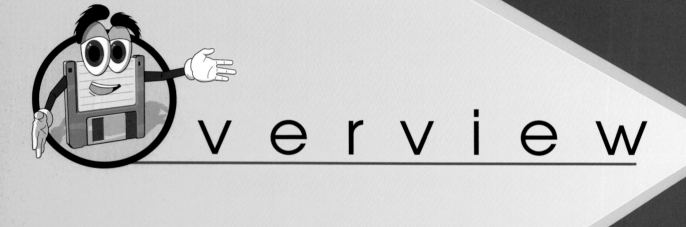

verview

EDIT YOUR DOCUMENTS

Insert Text

Delete Text

Undo Last Changes

Undelete Text

Move Text

Copy Text

Change the Case of Text

Work with Codes

In this chapter you will learn how to make changes to text in your document.

INSERT TEXT

INSERT A BLANK LINE

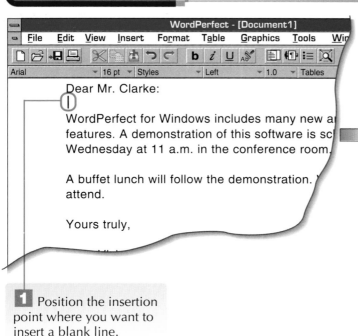

1 Position the insertion point where you want to insert a blank line.

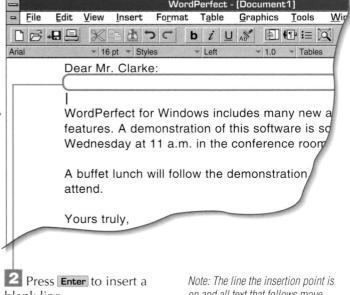

2 Press **Enter** to insert a blank line.

Note: The line the insertion point is on and all text that follows move down one line.

Getting Started	Edit Your Documents	Smart Editing	Save and Open Your Documents	Print Your Documents	Change Your Document Display	Using Multiple Documents

- **Insert Text**
- Delete Text
- Undo Last Changes
- Undelete Text
- Move Text
- Copy Text
- Change the Case of Text
- Work with Codes

IMPORTANT!

◆ Make sure you save your document to store it for future use. If you do not save your document, it will disappear when you turn off your computer.

Note: To save a document, refer to page 56.

SPLIT AND JOIN PARAGRAPHS

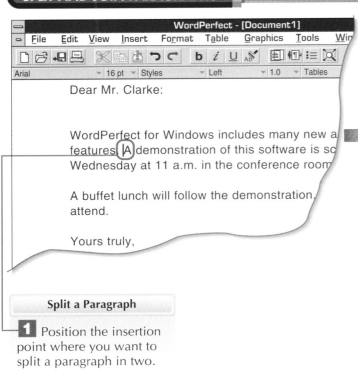

Split a Paragraph

1 Position the insertion point where you want to split a paragraph in two.

2 Press **Enter** and the paragraph splits in two.

3 To insert a blank line between the two paragraphs, press **Enter** again.

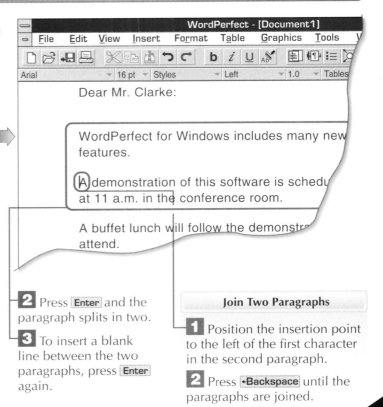

Join Two Paragraphs

1 Position the insertion point to the left of the first character in the second paragraph.

2 Press **+Backspace** until the paragraphs are joined.

INSERT TEXT

In the Insert mode, the text you type appears at the insertion point location. The existing text moves forward to make room for the new text.

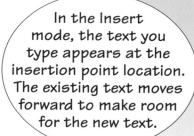

This sentence moves forward as you type.

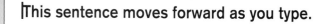

This sentence moves forward as you type.

INSERT TEXT

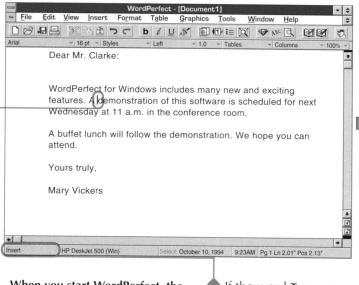

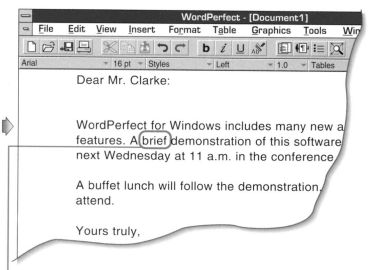

When you start WordPerfect, the program is in the Insert mode.

◆ If the word **Typeover** is displayed at the bottom of your screen, press **Insert**. This turns on the **Insert** mode.

1 Position the insertion point where you want to insert the new text.

2 Type the text you want to insert (example: **brief**).

3 To insert a blank space, press the **Spacebar**.

Note: The words to the right of the inserted text are pushed forward.

| Getting Started | **Edit Your Documents** | Smart Editing | Save and Open Your Documents | Print Your Documents | Change Your Document Display | Using Multiple Documents |

- **• Insert Text**
- • Delete Text
- • Undo Last Changes
- • Undelete Text
- • Move Text
- • Copy Text
- • Change the Case of Text
- • Work with Codes

In the Typeover mode, the text you type appears at the insertion point location. The new text replaces (types over) any existing text.

This sentence disappears as you type.

xxxxxxxxxxxxxxxxxxxpears as you type.

TYPEOVER TEXT

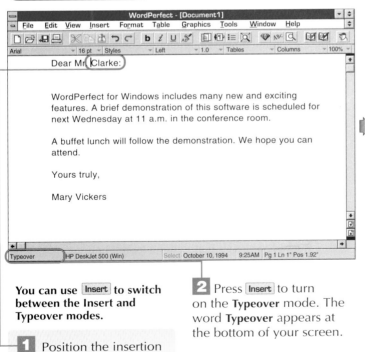

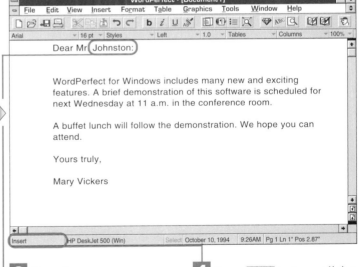

You can use Insert **to switch between the Insert and Typeover modes.**

1 Position the insertion point to the left of the first character you want to type over.

2 Press Insert to turn on the **Typeover** mode. The word **Typeover** appears at the bottom of your screen.

3 Type the text you want to replace the existing text (example: **Johnston:**).

4 Press Insert to turn off the **Typeover** mode. The word **Insert** appears at the bottom of your screen.

DELETE TEXT

You can use **Delete** to remove the character to the right of the insertion point. The remaining text moves to the left.

Delete **DELETE CHARACTERS**

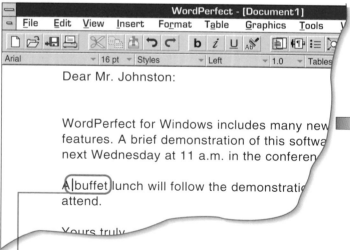

WordPerfect - [Document1]

File Edit View Insert Format Table Graphics Tools

Arial   16 pt   Styles   Left   1.0   Tables

Dear Mr. Johnston:

WordPerfect for Windows includes many new features. A brief demonstration of this softwa next Wednesday at 11 a.m. in the conferen

A buffet lunch will follow the demonstratio attend.

Yours truly,

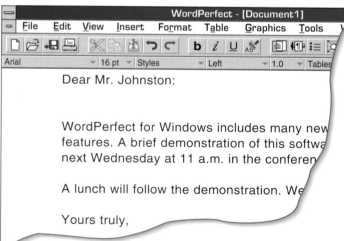

WordPerfect - [Document1]

File Edit View Insert Format Table Graphics Tools

Arial   16 pt   Styles   Left   1.0   Tables

Dear Mr. Johnston:

WordPerfect for Windows includes many new features. A brief demonstration of this softwa next Wednesday at 11 a.m. in the conferen

A lunch will follow the demonstration. We

Yours truly,

1 Position the insertion point to the left of the character you want to delete (example: **b** in buffet).

2 Press **Delete** once for each character you want to delete (example: press **Delete** seven times).

You can also use this key to delete characters. Position the insertion point to the **right** of the character(s) you want to delete and then press **◄Backspace**.

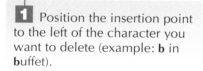

Getting
Started

**Edit Your
Documents**

Smart
Editing

Save and
Open Your
Documents

Print Your
Documents

Change Your
Document
Display

Using
Multiple
Documents

- Insert Text
- **Delete Text**
- Undo Last Changes
- Undelete Text

- Move Text
- Copy Text
- Change the Case of Text
- Work with Codes

You can use Delete
to remove the blank line
the insertion point is on.
The remaining text moves
up one line.

Delete — *DELETE A BLANK LINE*

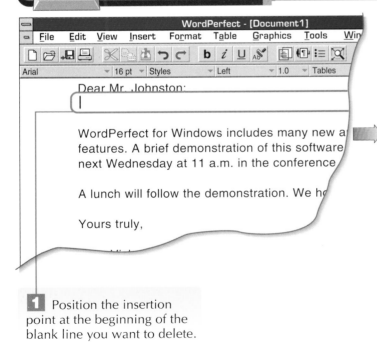

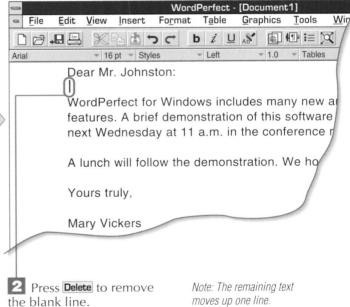

1 Position the insertion
point at the beginning of the
blank line you want to delete.

2 Press Delete to remove
the blank line.

*Note: The remaining text
moves up one line.*

DELETE TEXT | UNDO LAST CHANGES

You can use **Delete** to remove text you have selected. The remaining text moves up or to the left to fill the empty space.

Delete | DELETE SELECTED TEXT

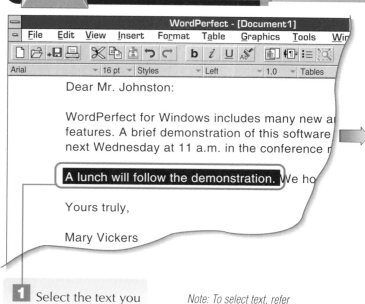

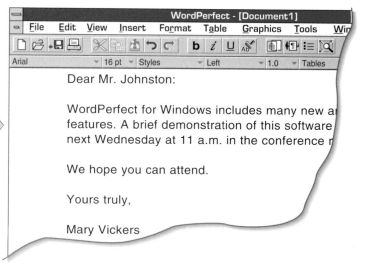

1 Select the text you want to delete.

Note: To select text, refer to page 16.

2 Press **Delete** to remove the text.

Getting
Started

**Edit Your
Documents**

Smart
Editing

Save and
Open Your
Documents

Print Your
Documents

Change Your
Document
Display

Using
Multiple
Documents

• Insert Text
• **Delete Text**
• **Undo Last Changes**
• Undelete Text

• Move Text
• Copy Text
• Change the Case of Text
• Work with Codes

WordPerfect remembers the last changes you made to your document. If you regret these changes, you can cancel them by using the Undo feature.

UNDO LAST CHANGES

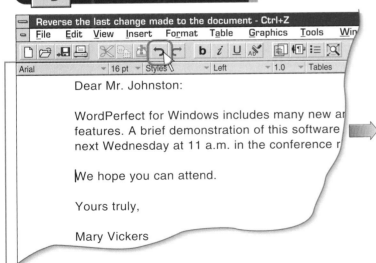

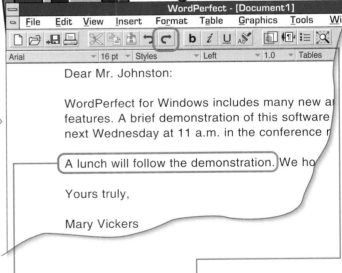

1 Move the mouse over ↶ and then press the left button.

Note: The Undo feature can cancel your last editing and formatting changes.

◆ WordPerfect cancels the last change you made to your document.

◆ Repeat step **1** to cancel previous changes you made.

◆ To reverse the results of using the Undo feature, move the mouse over ↷ and then press the left button.

29

UNDELETE TEXT

If you accidentally delete text, it is not permanently lost. WordPerfect remembers your last three text deletions and can restore them.

UNDELETE TEXT

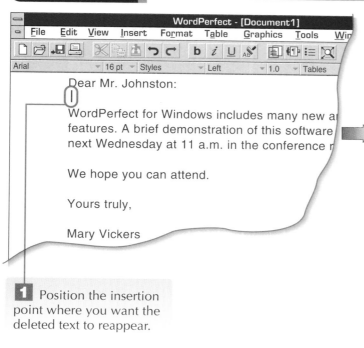

WordPerfect - [Document1]

File   Edit   View   Insert   Format   Table   Graphics   Tools   Win

Arial   16 pt   Styles   Left   1.0   Tables

Dear Mr. Johnston:

WordPerfect for Windows includes many new a
features. A brief demonstration of this software
next Wednesday at 11 a.m. in the conference r

We hope you can attend.

Yours truly,

Mary Vickers

1 Position the insertion point where you want the deleted text to reappear.

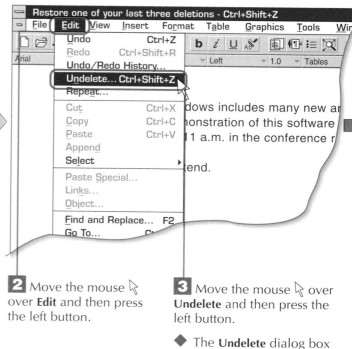

Restore one of your last three deletions - Ctrl+Shift+Z

File   Edit   View   Insert   Format   Table   Graphics   Tools   Win

Undo   Ctrl+Z
Redo   Ctrl+Shift+R
Undo/Redo History...
Undelete... Ctrl+Shift+Z
Repeat...

Cut   Ctrl+X
Copy   Ctrl+C
Paste   Ctrl+V
Append
Select

Paste Special...
Links...
Object...

Find and Replace...   F2
Go To...

2 Move the mouse over **Edit** and then press the left button.

3 Move the mouse over **Undelete** and then press the left button.

◆ The **Undelete** dialog box appears.

30

Getting Started	Edit Your Documents	Smart Editing	Save and Open Your Documents	Print Your Documents	Change Your Document Display	Using Multiple Documents

- Insert Text
- Delete Text
- Undo Last Changes
- **Undelete Text**
- Move Text
- Copy Text
- Change the Case of Text
- Work with Codes

It is important to understand the differences between the Undo and Undelete features.

Note: To use the **Undo** feature, refer to page 29.

UNDO

◆ Undo can restore the last changes you made to your document, including any editing or formatting change.

◆ Undo places deleted text where it was originally located in your document.

UNDELETE

◆ Undelete can restore your last three text deletions at any time.

◆ Undelete places deleted text at the location you specify in your document.

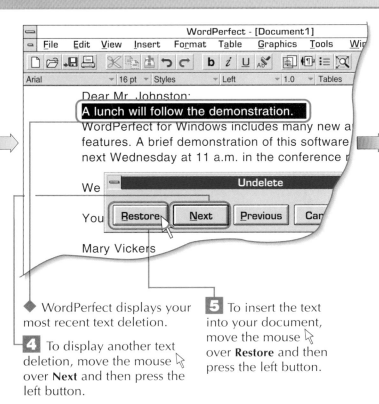

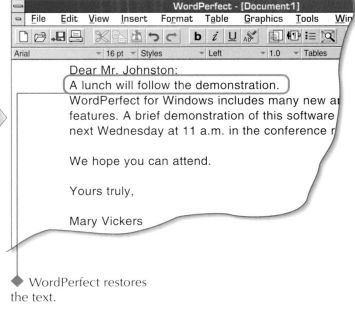

◆ WordPerfect displays your most recent text deletion.

4 To display another text deletion, move the mouse over **Next** and then press the left button.

Note: To cycle through your last three text deletions, repeat step **4**.

5 To insert the text into your document, move the mouse over **Restore** and then press the left button.

◆ WordPerfect restores the text.

MOVE TEXT

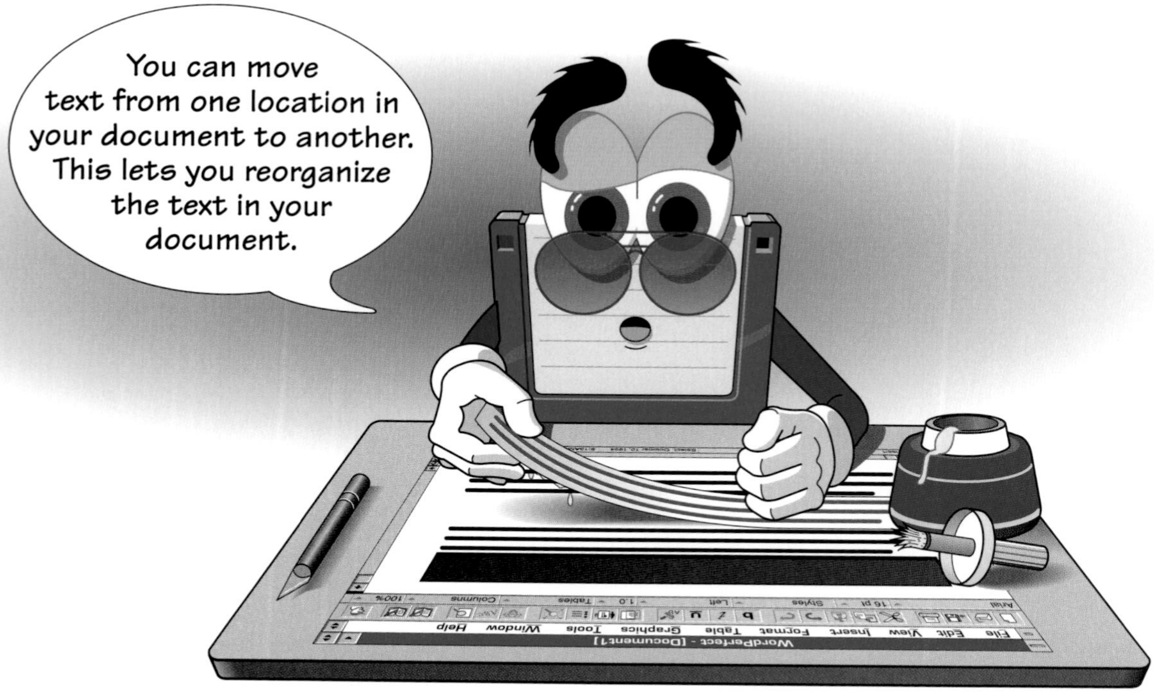
You can move text from one location in your document to another. This lets you reorganize the text in your document.

MOVE TEXT

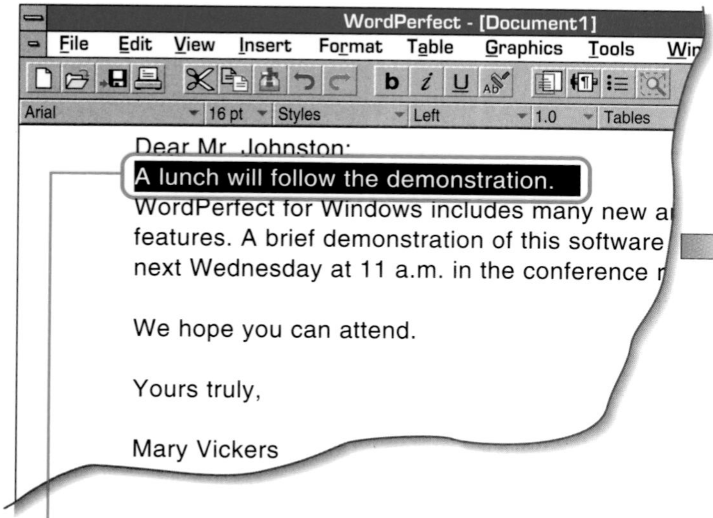
WordPerfect - [Document1]
File Edit View Insert Format Table Graphics Tools Win
Arial 16 pt Styles Left 1.0 Tables
Dear Mr. Johnston:
A lunch will follow the demonstration.
WordPerfect for Windows includes many new a
features. A brief demonstration of this software
next Wednesday at 11 a.m. in the conference r
We hope you can attend.
Yours truly,
Mary Vickers

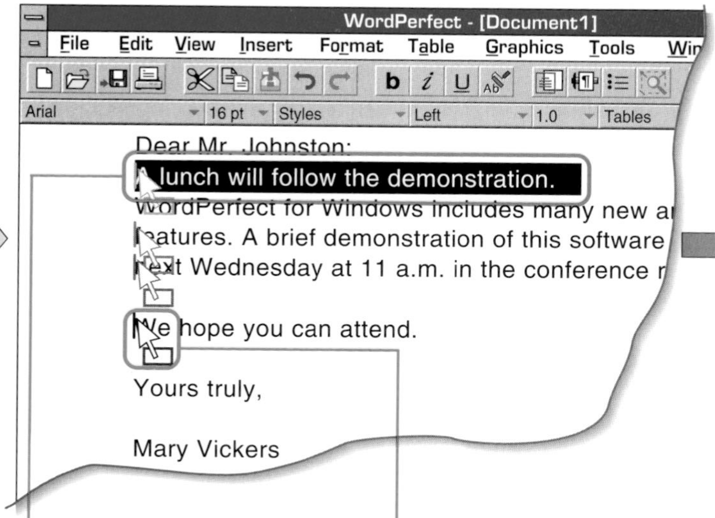
WordPerfect - [Document1]
File Edit View Insert Format Table Graphics Tools Win
Arial 16 pt Styles Left 1.0 Tables
Dear Mr. Johnston:
A lunch will follow the demonstration.
WordPerfect for Windows includes many new a
features. A brief demonstration of this software
next Wednesday at 11 a.m. in the conference r
We hope you can attend.
Yours truly,
Mary Vickers

1 Select the text you want to move.

Note: To select text, refer to page 16.

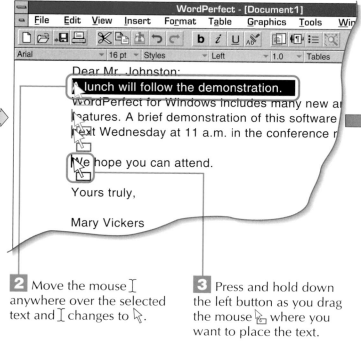

2 Move the mouse I anywhere over the selected text and I changes to ↖.

3 Press and hold down the left button as you drag the mouse where you want to place the text.

Note: The text will appear where the insertion point flashes on your screen.

Getting Started	Edit Your Documents	Smart Editing	Save and Open Your Documents	Print Your Documents	Change Your Document Display	Using Multiple Documents

- Insert Text
- Delete Text
- Undo Last Changes
- Undelete Text

- **Move Text**
- Copy Text
- Change the Case of Text
- Work with Codes

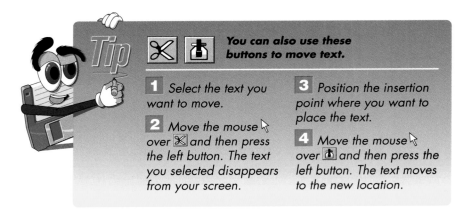

You can also use these buttons to move text.

1 Select the text you want to move.

2 Move the mouse over ✄ and then press the left button. The text you selected disappears from your screen.

3 Position the insertion point where you want to place the text.

4 Move the mouse over 🔲 and then press the left button. The text moves to the new location.

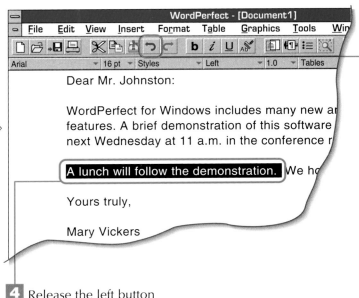

You can cancel the last change you made to your document.

◆ To move the text back to its original location, move the mouse ⯑ over ⤺ and then press the left button.

4 Release the left button and the text moves to the new location.

COPY TEXT

You can place a copy of text in a different location in your document. This will save you time since you do not have to retype the text.

COPY TEXT

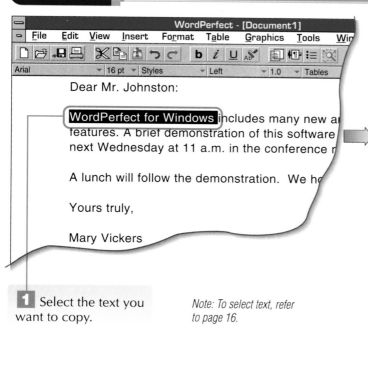

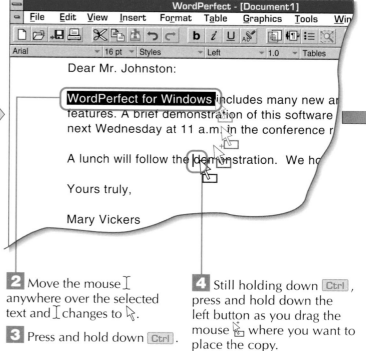

1 Select the text you want to copy.

Note: To select text, refer to page 16.

2 Move the mouse I anywhere over the selected text and I changes to ⌖.

3 Press and hold down `Ctrl`.

4 Still holding down `Ctrl`, press and hold down the left button as you drag the mouse ⌖ where you want to place the copy.

Note: The text will appear where the insertion point flashes on your screen.

34

Getting Started	Edit Your Documents	Smart Editing	Save and Open Your Documents	Print Your Documents	Change Your Document Display	Using Multiple Documents

- Insert Text
- Delete Text
- Undo Last Changes
- Undelete Text
- Move Text
- **Copy Text**
- Change the Case of Text
- Work with Codes

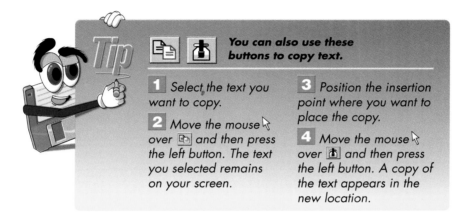

Tip

You can also use these buttons to copy text.

1 *Select the text you want to copy.*

2 *Move the mouse over and then press the left button. The text you selected remains on your screen.*

3 *Position the insertion point where you want to place the copy.*

4 *Move the mouse over and then press the left button. A copy of the text appears in the new location.*

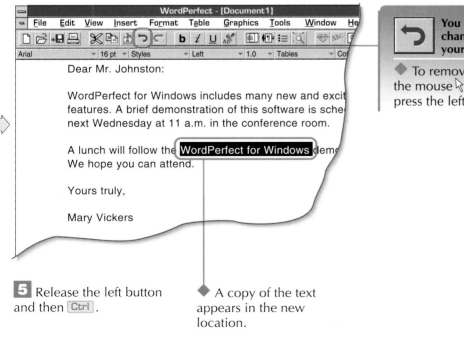

WordPerfect - [Document1]

File Edit View Insert Format Table Graphics Tools Window He

Arial 16 pt Styles Left 1.0 Tables Co

Dear Mr. Johnston:

WordPerfect for Windows includes many new and excit
features. A brief demonstration of this software is sche
next Wednesday at 11 a.m. in the conference room.

A lunch will follow the WordPerfect for Windows dem
We hope you can attend.

Yours truly,

Mary Vickers

You can cancel the last change you made to your document.

◆ To remove the copy, move the mouse over and then press the left button.

5 Release the left button and then Ctrl.

◆ A copy of the text appears in the new location.

CHANGE THE CASE OF TEXT

You can change the case of text in your document without retyping the text. WordPerfect offers three case options.

Lowercase
I wish to complain about this parrot

UPPERCASE
I WISH TO COMPLAIN ABOUT THIS PARROT

Initial Capitals
I Wish to Complain about this Parrot

CHANGE THE CASE OF TEXT

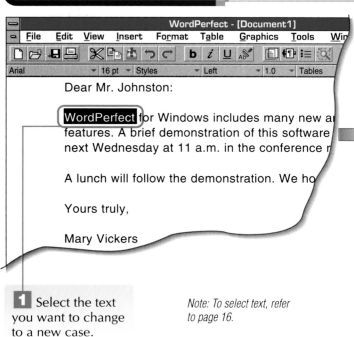

1 Select the text you want to change to a new case.

Note: To select text, refer to page 16.

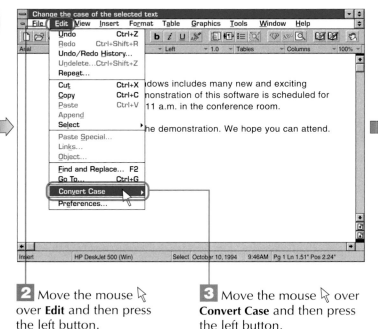

2 Move the mouse ▷ over **Edit** and then press the left button.

3 Move the mouse ▷ over **Convert Case** and then press the left button.

36

| Getting Started | **Edit Your Documents** | Smart Editing | Save and Open Your Documents | Print Your Documents | Change Your Document Display | Using Multiple Documents |

- Insert Text
- Delete Text
- Undo Last Changes
- Undelete Text

- Move Text
- Copy Text
- **Change the Case of Text**
- Work with Codes

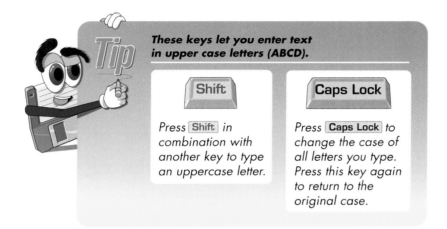

These keys let you enter text in upper case letters (ABCD).

Shift

Press **Shift** in combination with another key to type an uppercase letter.

Caps Lock

Press **Caps Lock** to change the case of all letters you type. Press this key again to return to the original case.

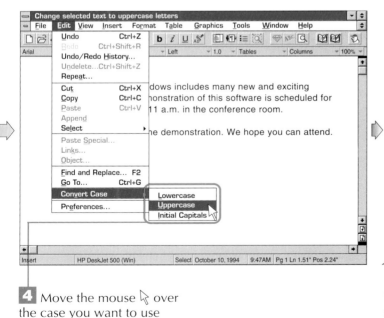

4 Move the mouse ⬦ over the case you want to use (example: **Uppercase**) and then press the left button.

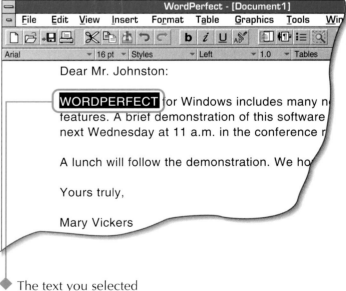

◆ The text you selected changes to the new case.

WORK WITH CODES

WordPerfect records your changes by inserting hidden codes in your document. You can display these codes to edit your document more efficiently.

DISPLAY CODES

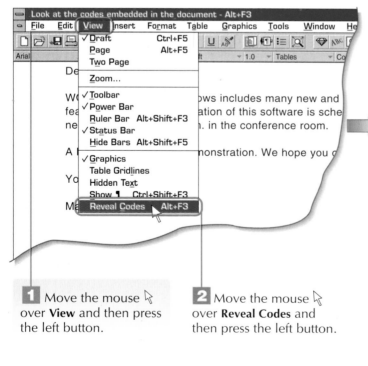

1 Move the mouse ⟍ over **View** and then press the left button.

2 Move the mouse ⟍ over **Reveal Codes** and then press the left button.

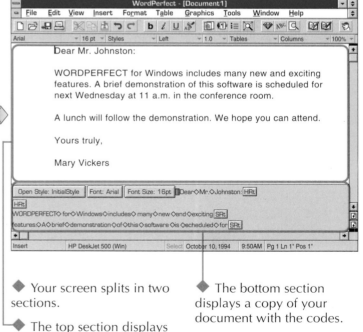

◆ Your screen splits in two sections.

◆ The top section displays your document.

◆ The bottom section displays a copy of your document with the codes.

*Note: To hide the codes, repeat steps **1** and **2**.*

38

Getting Started	Edit Your Documents	Smart Editing	Save and Open Your Documents	Print Your Documents	Change Your Document Display	Using Multiple Documents

- Insert Text
- Delete Text
- Undo Last Changes
- Undelete Text
- Move Text
- Copy Text
- Change the Case of Text
- **Work with Codes**

Tip

When you press `Enter` on your keyboard, WordPerfect inserts `HRt` in your document. This represents a **hard return**.

When you type text and it automatically wraps to the next line, WordPerfect inserts `SRt` in your document. This represents a **soft return**.

DELETE A CODE

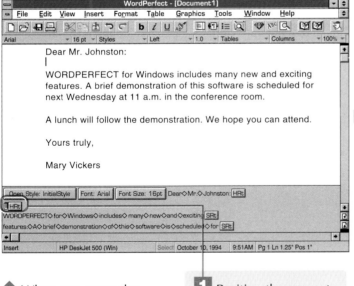

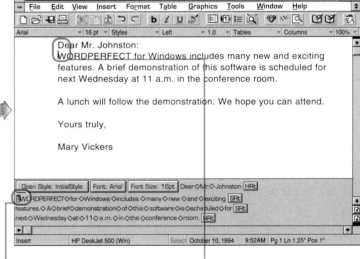

◆ When you move the insertion point in the top section, the cursor (❚) in the bottom section moves to the corresponding location.

1 Position the cursor to the left of the code you want to delete (example: `HRt`).

2 Press `Delete` on your keyboard.

◆ The code disappears from the bottom section of your screen.

◆ The top section of your screen displays the change (example: the blank line disappears).

*Note: To insert a blank line, refer to page 22. This will reinsert the **HRt** code in your document.*

39

SMART EDITING

Find and Replace Text

Using QuickCorrect

Check Spelling

Using the Thesaurus

Check Grammar

◇ In this chapter you will learn how to use WordPerfect's powerful editing features to improve the quality of your document.

FIND AND REPLACE TEXT

You can use the Find and Replace feature to locate every occurrence of a word or phrase in your document. You can then replace the word or phrase with new text. This is ideal if you have frequently misspelled a name.

FIND AND REPLACE TEXT

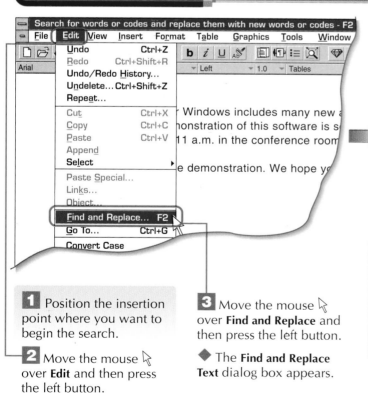

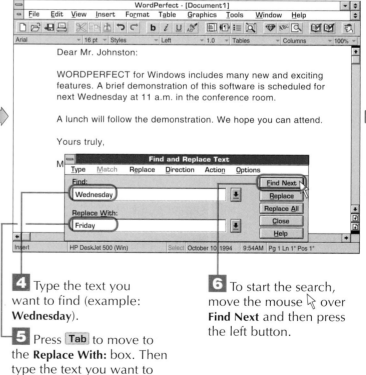

1 Position the insertion point where you want to begin the search.

2 Move the mouse over **Edit** and then press the left button.

3 Move the mouse over **Find and Replace** and then press the left button.

◆ The **Find and Replace Text** dialog box appears.

4 Type the text you want to find (example: **Wednesday**).

5 Press **Tab** to move to the **Replace With:** box. Then type the text you want to replace the searched word (example: **Friday**).

6 To start the search, move the mouse over **Find Next** and then press the left button.

Getting
Started

Edit Your
Documents

**Smart
Editing**

Save and
Open Your
Documents

Print Your
Documents

Change Your
Document
Display

Using
Multiple
Documents

• **Find and Replace Text**
• Using QuickCorrect
• Check Spelling
• Using the Thesaurus
• Check Grammar

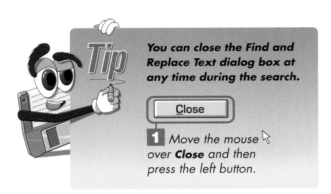

Tip

You can close the Find and Replace Text dialog box at any time during the search.

Close

1 Move the mouse over **Close** and then press the left button.

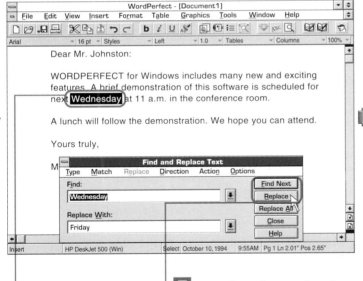

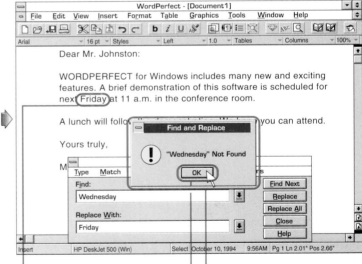

◆ WordPerfect highlights the first matching word it finds.

*Note: To replace the word and all other occurrences of the word in your document, move the mouse over **Replace All** and then press the left button.*

7 To replace the word and search for the next occurrence, move the mouse over **Replace** and then press the left button.

◆ To ignore the word and search for the next occurrence, move the mouse over **Find Next** and then press the left button.

◆ WordPerfect replaces the word and searches for the next occurrence.

8 Repeat step **7** for each matching word that WordPerfect finds.

◆ This dialog box appears when WordPerfect cannot find any more occurrences of the word in your document.

9 To close the dialog box, move the mouse over **OK** and then press the left button.

USING QUICKCORRECT

Replace	With
artic	arctic
comittee	committee
Febuary	February
july	July
recieve	receive
teh	the
wierd	weird

WordPerfect automatically corrects common spelling errors as you type. You can customize the QuickCorrect list to include words you often misspell.

ADD TEXT TO THE QUICKCORRECT LIST

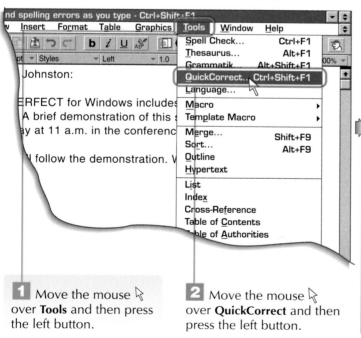

1 Move the mouse ⟨ over **Tools** and then press the left button.

2 Move the mouse ⟨ over **QuickCorrect** and then press the left button.

◆ The **QuickCorrect** dialog box appears.

3 Type the text you want WordPerfect to automatically correct every time you type it in a document (example: **repitition**).

4 Press **Tab** to move to the **With:** box. Then type the correct spelling of the word (example: **repetition**).

5 Move the mouse ⟨ over **Add Entry** and then press the left button.

44

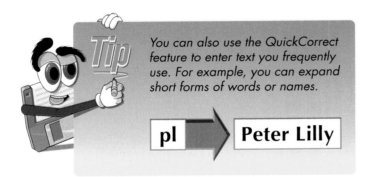

You can also use the QuickCorrect feature to enter text you frequently use. For example, you can expand short forms of words or names.

pl → **Peter Lilly**

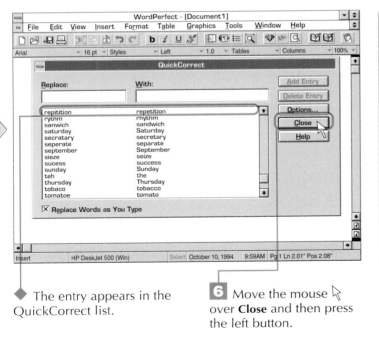

◆ The entry appears in the QuickCorrect list.

6 Move the mouse over **Close** and then press the left button.

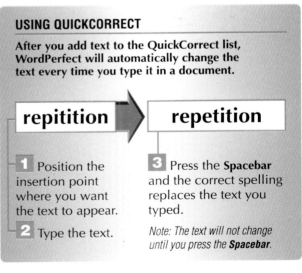

USING QUICKCORRECT

After you add text to the QuickCorrect list, WordPerfect will automatically change the text every time you type it in a document.

repitition → **repetition**

1 Position the insertion point where you want the text to appear.

2 Type the text.

3 Press the **Spacebar** and the correct spelling replaces the text you typed.

*Note: The text will not change until you press the **Spacebar**.*

CHECK SPELLING

You can use the Spelling feature to find and correct spelling errors in your document.

WordPerfect compares every word in your document to words in its dictionary. If a word does not exist in the dictionary, WordPerfect considers it misspelled.

CHECK SPELLING

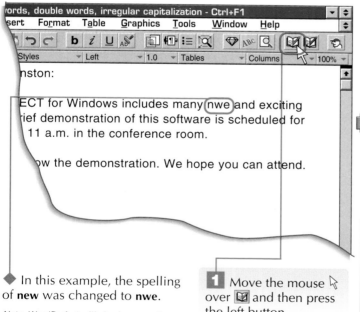

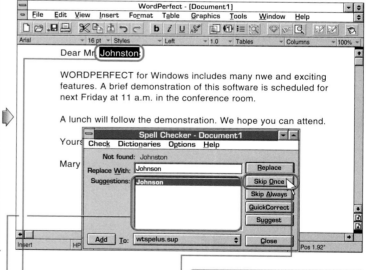

◆ In this example, the spelling of **new** was changed to **nwe**.

Note: WordPerfect will check your entire document. To spell check a section of your document, select the text before performing step **1**. *To select text, refer to page 16.*

1 Move the mouse ⌖ over 🖫 and then press the left button.

◆ The **Spell Checker** dialog box appears.

◆ WordPerfect highlights the first word it does not recognize (example: **Johnston**).

◆ The **Suggestions**: box displays alternative spellings.

Skip Misspelled Word

2 To skip the word and continue checking your document, move the mouse ⌖ over **Skip Once** and then press the left button.

*Note: To skip the word and all other occurrences of the word in your document, move the mouse ⌖ over **Skip Always** and then press the left button.*

46

Getting Started	Edit Your Documents	**Smart Editing**	Save and Open Your Documents	Print Your Documents	Change Your Document Display	Using Multiple Documents

- Find and Replace Text
- Using QuickCorrect
- **Check Spelling**
- Using the Thesaurus
- Check Grammar

*The Spelling feature will **not** find a correctly spelled word used in the wrong context.*

Example:

> *The girl is **sit** years old.*

You must review your document carefully to find this type of error.

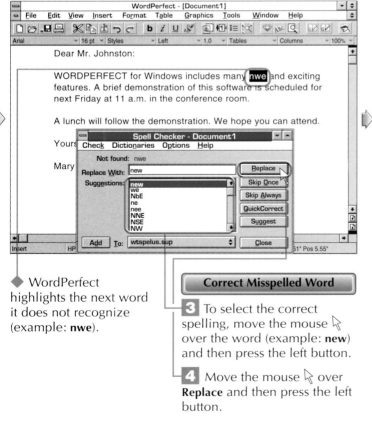

◆ WordPerfect highlights the next word it does not recognize (example: **nwe**).

Correct Misspelled Word

3 To select the correct spelling, move the mouse over the word (example: **new**) and then press the left button.

4 Move the mouse over **Replace** and then press the left button.

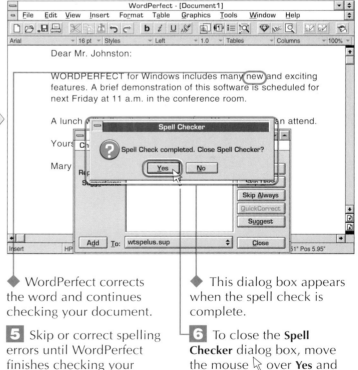

◆ WordPerfect corrects the word and continues checking your document.

5 Skip or correct spelling errors until WordPerfect finishes checking your document.

◆ This dialog box appears when the spell check is complete.

6 To close the **Spell Checker** dialog box, move the mouse over **Yes** and then press the left button.

USING THE THESAURUS

You can use the Thesaurus to add variety to your writing. This feature lets you replace a word in your document with one that is more suitable.

USING THE THESAURUS

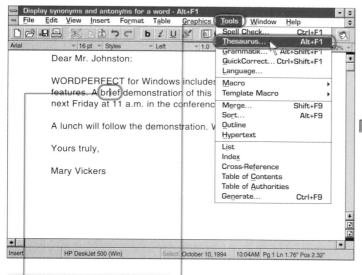

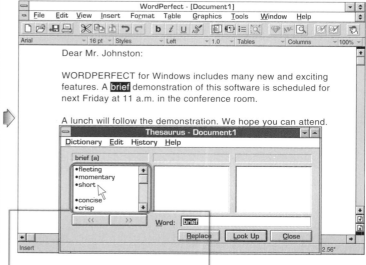

1 Position the insertion point anywhere in the word you want to look up (example: **brief**).

2 Move the mouse ⍙ over **Tools** and then press the left button.

3 Move the mouse ⍙ over **Thesaurus** and then press the left button.

◆ This area displays a list of alternative words.

Note: To view additional words in the list, use the scroll bar. For more information, refer to page 15.

4 To display terms related to a word in the list, move the mouse ⍙ over the word and then quickly press the left button twice.

Getting Started	Edit Your Documents	Smart Editing	Save and Open Your Documents	Print Your Documents	Change Your Document Display	Using Multiple Documents

- Find and Replace Text
- Using QuickCorrect
- Check Spelling
- **Using the Thesaurus**
- Check Grammar

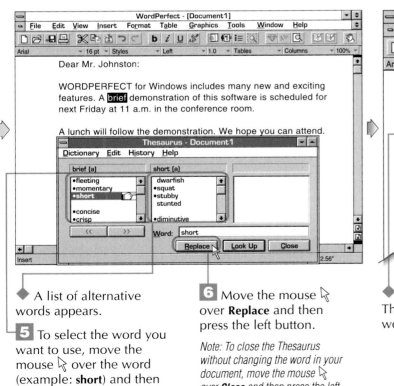

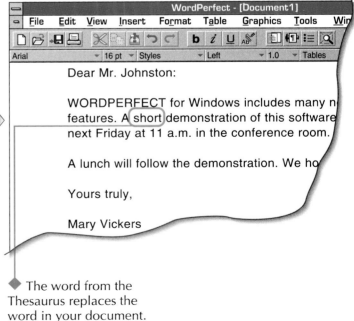

◆ A list of alternative words appears.

5 To select the word you want to use, move the mouse over the word (example: **short**) and then press the left button.

6 Move the mouse over **Replace** and then press the left button.

*Note: To close the Thesaurus without changing the word in your document, move the mouse over **Close** and then press the left button.*

◆ The word from the Thesaurus replaces the word in your document.

CHECK GRAMMAR

You can use the Grammar feature to check for grammar and spelling errors. This will improve the accuracy of your document.

CHECK GRAMMAR

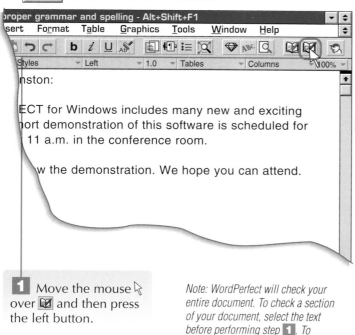

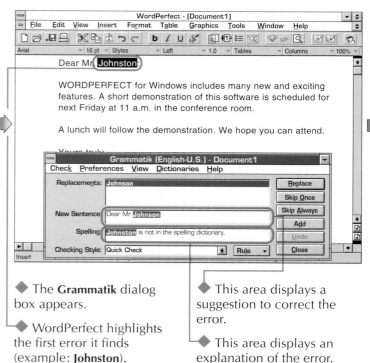

1 Move the mouse over ☑ and then press the left button.

*Note: WordPerfect will check your entire document. To check a section of your document, select the text before performing step **1**. To select text, refer to page 16.*

◆ The **Grammatik** dialog box appears.

◆ WordPerfect highlights the first error it finds (example: **Johnston**).

◆ This area displays a suggestion to correct the error.

◆ This area displays an explanation of the error.

Tip

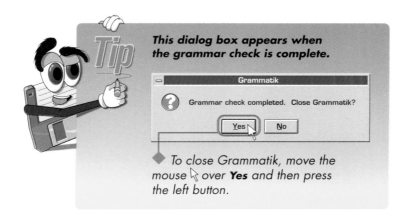

This dialog box appears when the grammar check is complete.

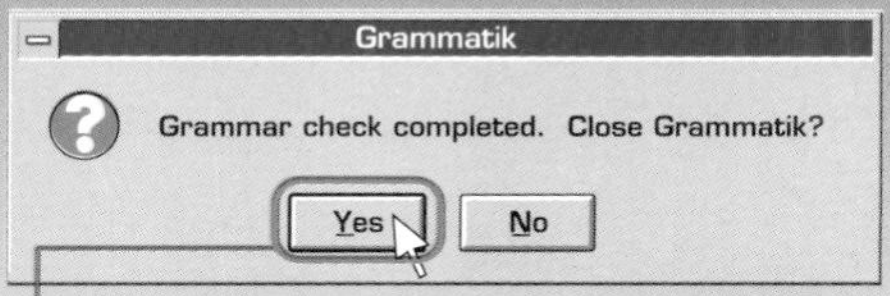
Grammatik
Grammar check completed. Close Grammatik?
Yes
No

◆ *To close Grammatik, move the mouse over **Yes** and then press the left button.*

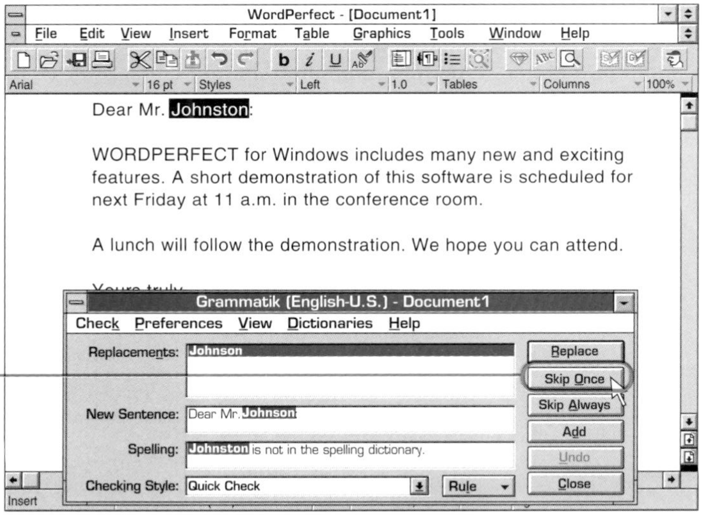
WordPerfect - [Document1]
File Edit View Insert Format Table Graphics Tools Window Help
Dear Mr. Johnston:
WORDPERFECT for Windows includes many new and exciting features. A short demonstration of this software is scheduled for next Friday at 11 a.m. in the conference room.
A lunch will follow the demonstration. We hope you can attend.
Grammatik (English-U.S.) - Document1
Check Preferences View Dictionaries Help
Replacements: Johnson
New Sentence: Dear Mr. Johnson:
Spelling: Johnston is not in the spelling dictionary.
Checking Style: Quick Check
Rule
Replace
Skip Once
Skip Always
Add
Undo
Close

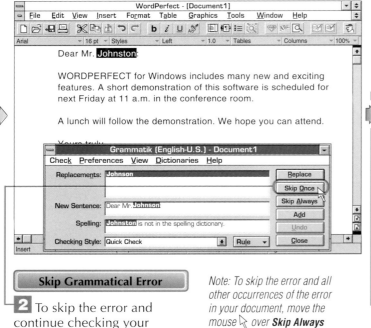

Skip Grammatical Error

2 To skip the error and continue checking your document, move the mouse over **Skip Once** and then press the left button.

*Note: To skip the error and all other occurrences of the error in your document, move the mouse over **Skip Always** and then press the left button.*

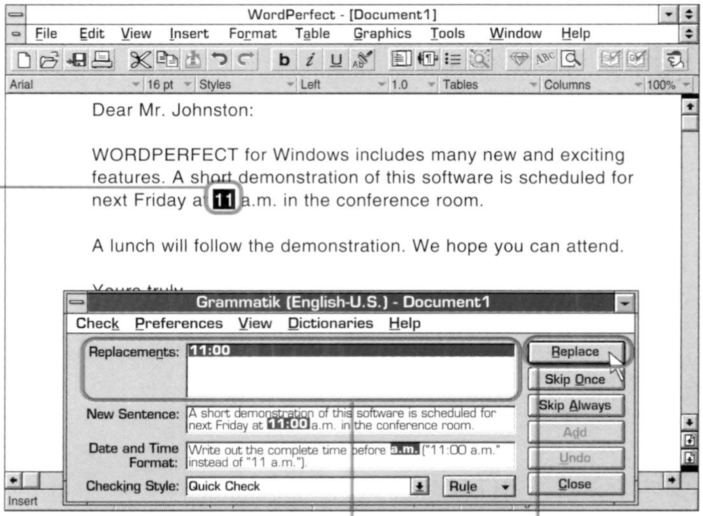
WordPerfect - [Document1]
File Edit View Insert Format Table Graphics Tools Window Help
Dear Mr. Johnston:
WORDPERFECT for Windows includes many new and exciting features. A short demonstration of this software is scheduled for next Friday at 11 a.m. in the conference room.
A lunch will follow the demonstration. We hope you can attend.
Grammatik (English-U.S.) - Document1
Check Preferences View Dictionaries Help
Replacements: 11:00
New Sentence: A short demonstration of this software is scheduled for next Friday at 11:00 a.m. in the conference room.
Date and Time Format: Write out the complete time before a.m. ("11:00 a.m." instead of "11 a.m.").
Checking Style: Quick Check
Rule
Replace
Skip Once
Skip Always
Add
Undo
Close

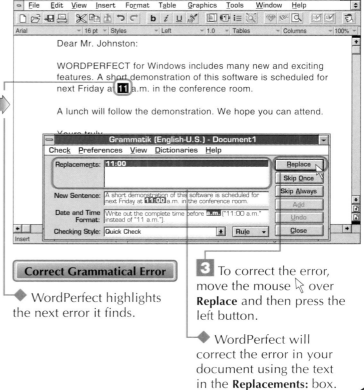

Correct Grammatical Error

◆ WordPerfect highlights the next error it finds.

3 To correct the error, move the mouse over **Replace** and then press the left button.

◆ WordPerfect will correct the error in your document using the text in the **Replacements:** box.

Overview

SAVE AND OPEN YOUR DOCUMENTS

Introduction

Save a New Document

Save a Document to a Diskette

Exit WordPerfect

Open a Document

Find a Document

◇ In this chapter you will learn how to save your work and exit WordPerfect. You will also learn how to find and open your documents.

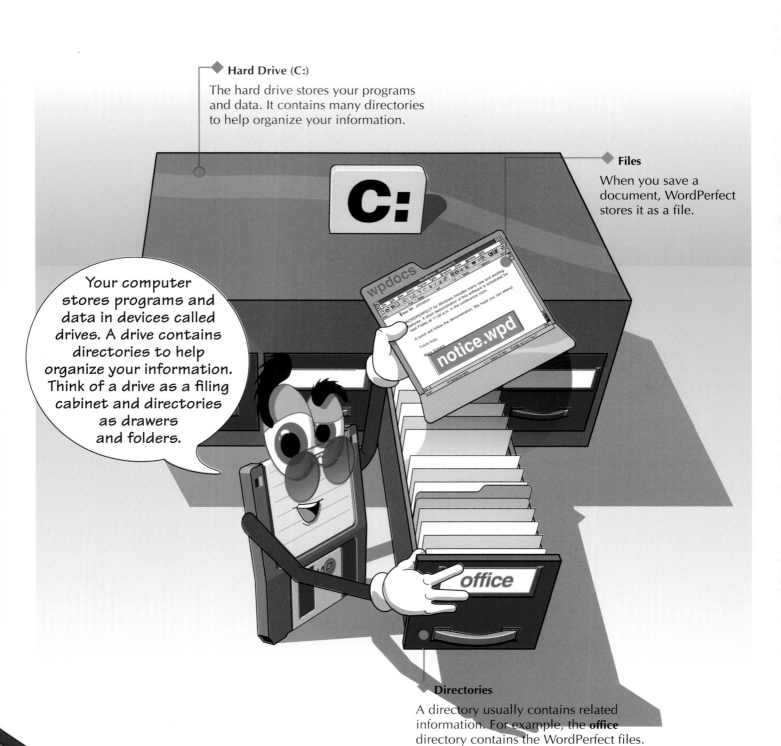

Hard Drive (C:)

The hard drive stores your programs and data. It contains many directories to help organize your information.

Files

When you save a document, WordPerfect stores it as a file.

Your computer stores programs and data in devices called drives. A drive contains directories to help organize your information. Think of a drive as a filing cabinet and directories as drawers and folders.

Directories

A directory usually contains related information. For example, the **office** directory contains the WordPerfect files.

INTRODUCTION TO WORDPERFECT

| Getting Started | Edit Your Documents | Smart Editing | **Save and Open Your Documents** | Print Your Documents | Change Your Document Display | Using Multiple Documents |

- **Introduction**
- Save a New Document
- Save a Document to a Diskette
- Exit WordPerfect
- Open a Document
- Find a Document

Most computers have one hard drive and one or two floppy drives to store information.

Hard drive (C:)

◆ The hard drive magnetically stores information inside your computer. It is called drive **C**.

*Note: Your computer may be set up to have additional hard drives (example: drive **D**).*

Floppy drives (A: and B:)

◆ A floppy drive stores information on removable diskettes (or floppy disks). A diskette operates slower and stores less data than a hard drive.

Diskettes are used to:
- Load new programs.
- Store backup copies of data.
- Transfer data to other computers.

If your computer has only one floppy drive, it is called drive **A**.

If your computer has two floppy drives, the second drive is called drive **B**.

SAVE A NEW DOCUMENT

You should save your document to store it for future use. This enables you to later retrieve the document for reviewing or editing purposes.

 SAVE A NEW DOCUMENT

A filename consists of two parts: a name and an extension. You must separate these parts with a period.

notice ● wpd

◆ **Name**

The name should describe the contents of a document. It can have up to eight characters.

◆ **Period**

A period must separate the name and the extension.

◆ **Extension**

The extension identifies the program you used to create the document. It can have up to three characters.

*Note: **wpd** stands for "WordPerfect document."*

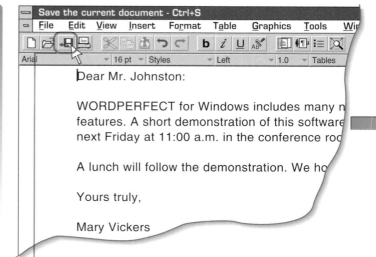

1 Move the mouse ⌖ over 🖫 and then press the left button.

◆ The **Save As** dialog box appears.

*Note: If you previously saved your document, the **Save As** dialog box will **not** appear since you have already named the document.*

Getting Started	Edit Your Documents	Smart Editing	**Save and Open Your Documents**	Print Your Documents	Change Your Document Display	Using Multiple Documents

- Introduction
- **Save a New Document**
- Save a Document to a Diskette

- Exit WordPerfect
- Open a Document
- Find a Document

Rules for Naming a Document

A filename *can* contain the following characters:

- The letters A to Z
- The numbers 0 to 9
- The symbols
  _ ^ $ ~ ! # % & { } @ ( )

A filename *cannot* contain the following characters:

- A comma (,)
- A blank space
- The symbols
  + = \ / ? < > *[ ] : ; |

Each document in a directory must have a unique name.

letter.wpd
note1q.wpd
test.wpd
training.wpd

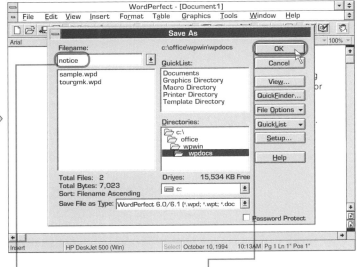

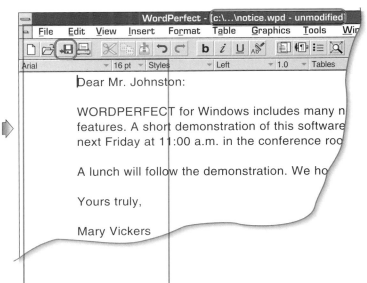

2 Type a name for your document (example: **notice**).

*Note: To make it easier to find your document later on, do not type an extension. WordPerfect will automatically add the **wpd** extension to the filename.*

3 Move the mouse ⌖ over **OK** and then press the left button.

◆ WordPerfect saves your document and displays the name at the top of your screen.

◆ You should save your document every 5 to 10 minutes to store any changes made since the last time you saved the document. To save changes, move the mouse ⌖ over 🖫 and then press the left button.

SAVE A DOCUMENT TO A DISKETTE

> If you want to give your colleagues a copy of a document, you can save the document to a diskette. They can then review the document on their own computers.

SAVE A DOCUMENT TO A DISKETTE

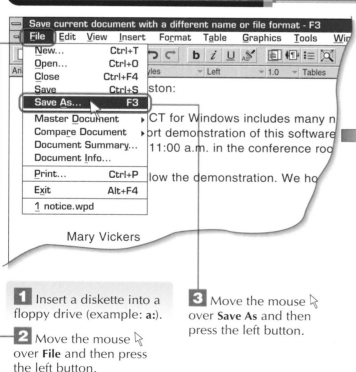

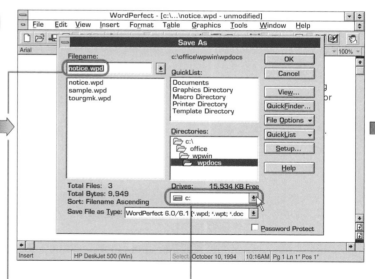

1 Insert a diskette into a floppy drive (example: **a:**).

2 Move the mouse ⬉ over **File** and then press the left button.

3 Move the mouse ⬉ over **Save As** and then press the left button.

◆ The **Save As** dialog box appears.

4 The **Filename:** box displays the current filename. To save your document with a different name, type a new name.

◆ The **Drives:** box displays the current drive (example: **c:**).

5 To save the document to a diskette, move the mouse ⬉ over ⬇ in the **Drives:** box and then press the left button.

SAVE A DOCUMENT WITH A NEW NAME

After you save your document, you may want to make additional changes. In case you regret any of these changes, you can keep a copy of the old version by saving the revised document with a new name.

1 Perform steps **2** to **4** below.

2 Move the mouse ⬚ over **OK** and then press the left button.

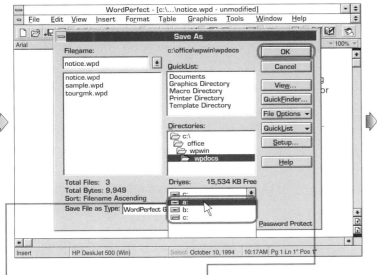

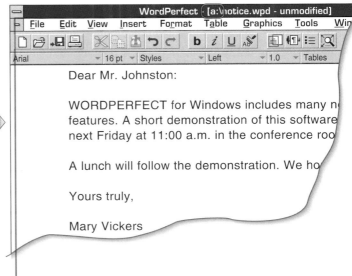

◆ A list of the available drives for the computer appears.

6 Move the mouse ⬚ over the drive you want to use (example: **a:**) and then press the left button.

7 To save your document, move the mouse ⬚ over **OK** and then press the left button.

◆ WordPerfect saves your document to the floppy drive (example: **a:**).

When you finish using WordPerfect, you can exit the program to return to the Windows Program Manager.

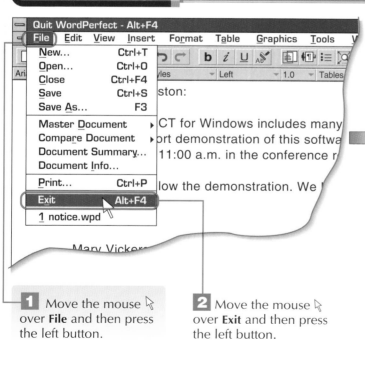

Quit WordPerfect - Alt+F4

File	Edit	View	Insert	Format	Table	Graphics	Tools

New...	Ctrl+T
Open...	Ctrl+O
Close	Ctrl+F4
Save	Ctrl+S
Save As...	F3
Master Document	▶
Compare Document	▶
Document Summary...	
Document Info...	
Print...	Ctrl+P
Exit	Alt+F4
1 notice.wpd	

1 Move the mouse over **File** and then press the left button.

2 Move the mouse over **Exit** and then press the left button.

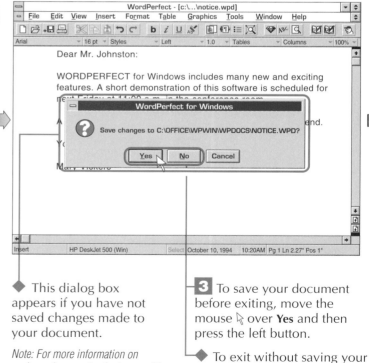

WordPerfect - [c:\...\notice.wpd]

| File | Edit | View | Insert | Format | Table | Graphics | Tools | Window | Help |

Arial   16 pt   Styles   Left   1.0   Tables   Columns   100%

Dear Mr. Johnston:

WORDPERFECT for Windows includes many new and exciting features. A short demonstration of this software is scheduled for

WordPerfect for Windows

? Save changes to C:\OFFICE\WPWIN\WPDOCS\NOTICE.WPD?

Yes   No   Cancel

Insert   HP DeskJet 500 (Win)   Select October 10, 1994   10:20AM Pg 1 Ln 2.27" Pos 1"

◆ This dialog box appears if you have not saved changes made to your document.

Note: For more information on saving a document, refer to page 56.

3 To save your document before exiting, move the mouse over **Yes** and then press the left button.

◆ To exit without saving your document, move the mouse over **No** and then press the left button.

Getting
Started

Edit Your
Documents

Smart
Editing

**Save and
Open Your
Documents**

Print Your
Documents

Change Your
Document
Display

Using
Multiple
Documents

- Introduction
- Save a New Document
- Save a Document to a Diskette

- **Exit WordPerfect**
- Open a Document
- Find a Document

IMPORTANT!

You must always exit
WordPerfect and Windows
before turning off your
computer. Failure to do so
may result in damage or loss
of valuable information.

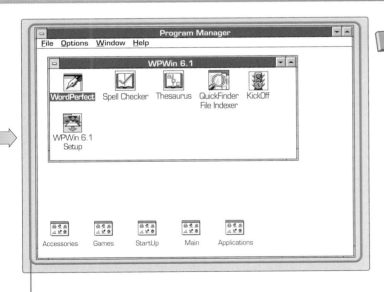

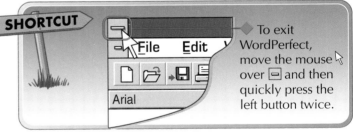

SHORTCUT

To exit
WordPerfect,
move the mouse
over ⊟ and then
quickly press the
left button twice.

◆ The **Program Manager**
window appears.

*Note: To restart WordPerfect,
refer to page 6.*

OPEN A DOCUMENT

You can open a saved document and display it on your screen. This lets you view and make changes to your document.

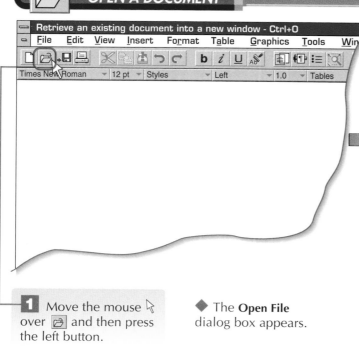

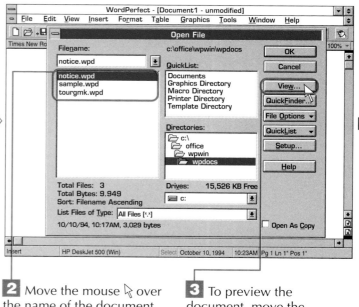

1 Move the mouse ⟍ over ⟋ and then press the left button.

◆ The **Open File** dialog box appears.

2 Move the mouse ⟍ over the name of the document you want to open (example: **notice.wpd**) and then press the left button.

3 To preview the document, move the mouse ⟍ over **View** and then press the left button.

| Getting Started | Edit Your Documents | Smart Editing | Save and Open Your Documents | Print Your Documents | Change Your Document Display | Using Multiple Documents |

- Introduction
- Save a New Document
- Save a Document to a Diskette
- Exit WordPerfect
- **Open a Document**
- Find a Document

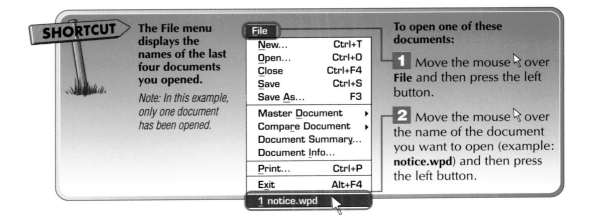

SHORTCUT

The File menu displays the names of the last four documents you opened.

Note: In this example, only one document has been opened.

File
New...	Ctrl+T
Open...	Ctrl+O
Close	Ctrl+F4
Save	Ctrl+S
Save As...	F3
Master Document	▶
Compare Document	▶
Document Summary...	
Document Info...	
Print...	Ctrl+P
Exit	Alt+F4
1 notice.wpd	

To open one of these documents:

1 Move the mouse ⬡ over **File** and then press the left button.

2 Move the mouse ⬡ over the name of the document you want to open (example: **notice.wpd**) and then press the left button.

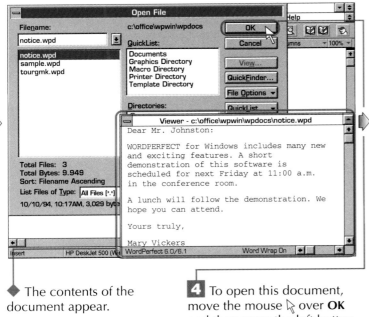

◆ The contents of the document appear.

Note: To view the contents of another document, repeat step 2.

4 To open this document, move the mouse ⬡ over **OK** and then press the left button.

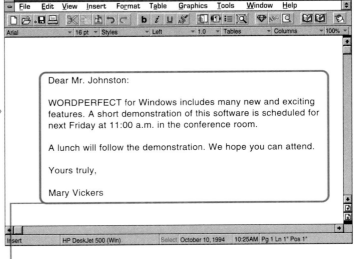

◆ WordPerfect opens the document and displays it on your screen. You can now make changes to the document.

FIND A DOCUMENT

If you cannot remember the name or location of the document you want to open, you can use QuickFinder to search for the document.

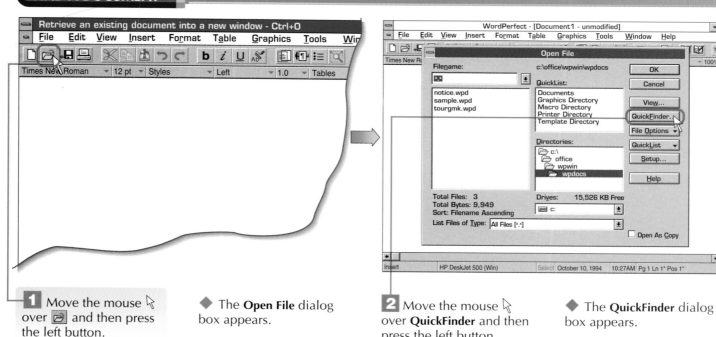

1 Move the mouse ⌖ over 📂 and then press the left button.

◆ The **Open File** dialog box appears.

2 Move the mouse ⌖ over **QuickFinder** and then press the left button.

◆ The **QuickFinder** dialog box appears.

64

INTRODUCTION TO WORDPERFECT

| Getting Started | Edit Your Documents | Smart Editing | Save and Open Your Documents | Print Your Documents | Change Your Document Display | Using Multiple Documents |

• Introduction
• Save a New Document
• Save a Document to a Diskette

• Exit WordPerfect
• Open a Document
• **Find a Document**

To cancel the search at any time, press Esc on your keyboard twice.

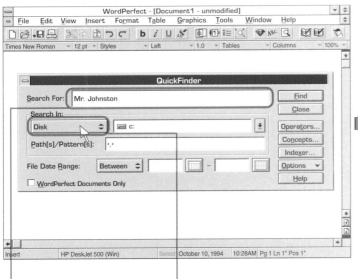

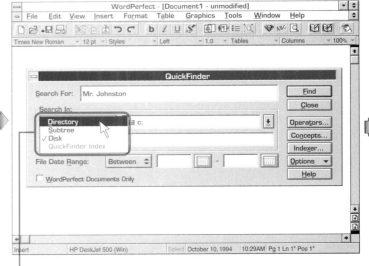

3 If you know a word or phrase in the document you want to find, type the text.

Note: If you do not know a word or phrase in the document, leave this area blank.

◆ This box displays the area WordPerfect will search.

4 To search another area, move the mouse ↕ over this box and then press and hold down the left button.

5 Still holding down the left button, move the mouse ↕ over the area you want to search (example: **Directory**). Then release the button.

To continue, refer to the next page.

Directory

Searches the current directory.

Subtree

Searches the current directory and all of its subdirectories.

Disk

Searches all directories and subdirectories on the current drive.

65

When the search is complete, WordPerfect will list the names of the documents it found. You can then preview the documents before opening the one you want to work with.

FIND A DOCUMENT (CONTINUED)

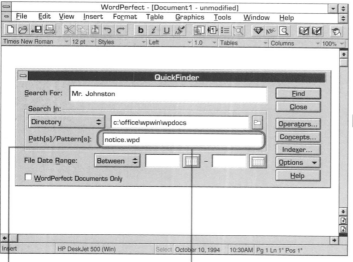

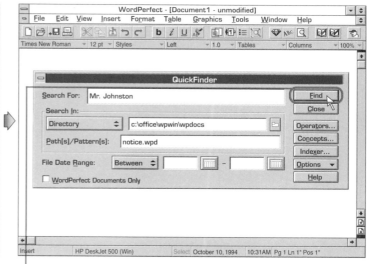

6 If you know the name of the document you want to find, move the mouse ⌶ over this box and then press the left button.

Note: If you do not know the name of the document, skip to step 8.

7 Press **◆Backspace** or **Delete** to remove the existing text. Then type the name of the document.

8 To start the search, move the mouse Ⓚ over **Find** and then press the left button.

Getting Started	Edit Your Documents	Smart Editing	**Save and Open Your Documents**	Print Your Documents	Change Your Document Display	Using Multiple Documents

- Introduction
- Save a New Document
- Save a Document to a Diskette

- Exit WordPerfect
- Open a Document
- **Find a Document**

If you know part of the name of the document you want to find, you can use the (*) wildcard character to search for the document.

The asterisk (*) represents one or more characters in a document name.

Examples:

notice*.*	Finds all documents starting with **notice**
*.wpd	Finds all documents with the **wpd** extension
.	Finds all documents

Note: You can enter this information in steps **6** and **7** on page 66.

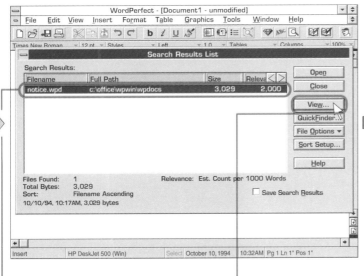

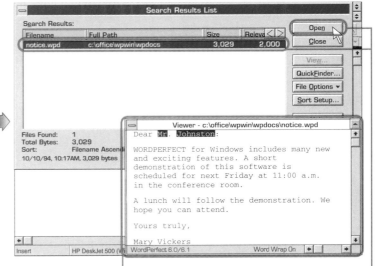

◆ The **Search Results List** dialog box appears displaying the names of the documents WordPerfect found.

9 To preview the contents of a document, move the mouse ⍹ over the document name and then press the left button.

10 Move the mouse ⍹ over **View** and then press the left button.

◆ The contents of the document you selected appear.

Note: Repeat step **9** for each document you want to view.

11 To open a document, move the mouse ⍹ over the name of the document and then press the left button.

12 Move the mouse ⍹ over **Open** and then press the left button.

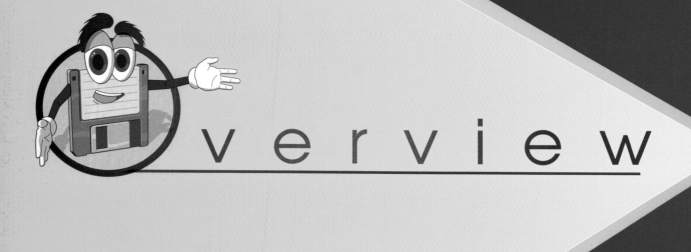

verview

PRINT YOUR DOCUMENTS

Display Document Information

Select a Printer

Print a Document

Print an Envelope

Print Labels

In this chapter you will learn how to print documents, envelopes and labels.

Before printing a document, you can display the word count, number of pages and other information about the document.

DISPLAY DOCUMENT INFORMATION

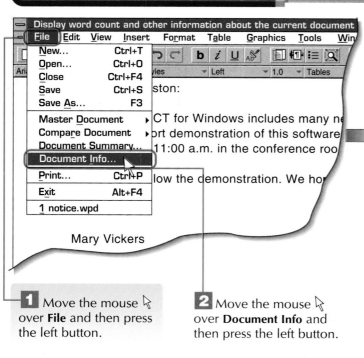

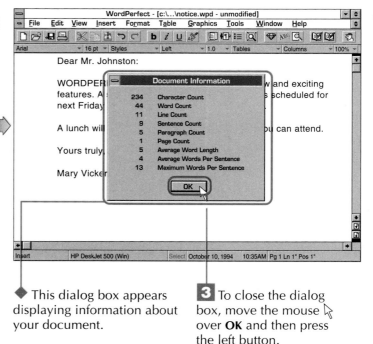

1 Move the mouse over **File** and then press the left button.

2 Move the mouse over **Document Info** and then press the left button.

◆ This dialog box appears displaying information about your document.

3 To close the dialog box, move the mouse over **OK** and then press the left button.

Getting
Started

Edit Your
Documents

Smart
Editing

Save and
Open Your
Documents

**Print Your
Documents**

Change Your
Document
Display

Using
Multiple
Documents

- **Display Document Information**
- **Select a Printer**
- Print a Document
- Print an Envelope
- Print Labels

If your computer is connected to more than one printer, you can easily switch to the printer you want to use.

SELECT A PRINTER

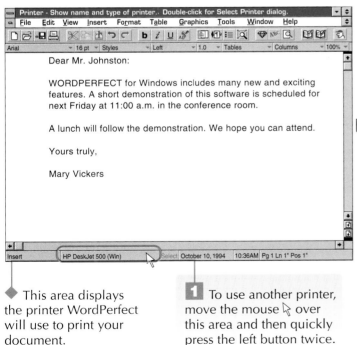

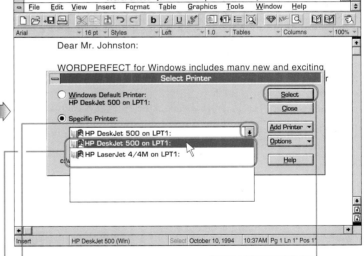

◆ This area displays the printer WordPerfect will use to print your document.

1 To use another printer, move the mouse ⬚ over this area and then quickly press the left button twice.

◆ The **Select Printer** dialog box appears.

2 To select another printer, move the mouse ⬚ over ⬇ and then press the left button.

3 Move the mouse ⬚ over the name of the printer you want to use and then press the left button.

4 Move the mouse ⬚ over **Select** and then press the left button.

PRINT A DOCUMENT

> You can print a single page, specific pages or your entire document.

PRINT A DOCUMENT

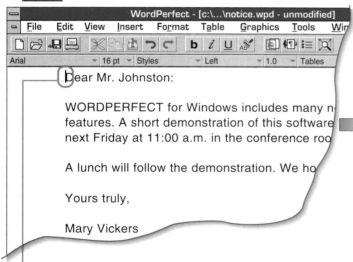

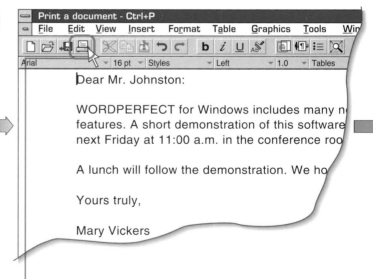

1 To print your entire document, position the insertion point anywhere in the document.

◆ To print a single page, position the insertion point anywhere on the page.

◆ To print a section of text, select the text you want to print.

Note: To select text, refer to page 16.

2 Move the mouse ⌖ over and then press the left button.

| Getting Started | Edit Your Documents | Smart Editing | Save and Open Your Documents | **Print Your Documents** | Change Your Document Display | Using Multiple Documents |

- Display Document Information
- Select a Printer
- **Print a Document**
- Print an Envelope
- Print Labels

MULTIPLE PAGES

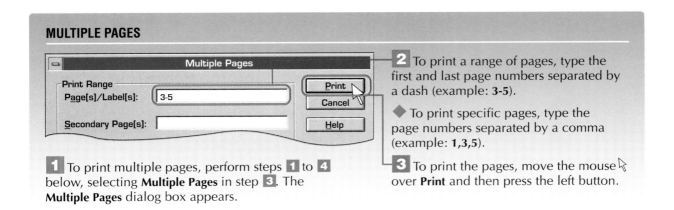

2 To print a range of pages, type the first and last page numbers separated by a dash (example: **3-5**).

◆ To print specific pages, type the page numbers separated by a comma (example: **1,3,5**).

1 To print multiple pages, perform steps **1** to **4** below, selecting **Multiple Pages** in step **3**. The **Multiple Pages** dialog box appears.

3 To print the pages, move the mouse ▷ over **Print** and then press the left button.

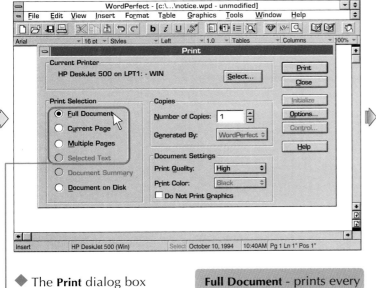

◆ The **Print** dialog box appears.

3 Move the mouse ▷ over the print selection you want to use and then press the left button (○ changes to ●).

Full Document - prints every page in the document.

Current Page - prints the page containing the insertion point.

Multiple Pages - prints the pages you specify.

Selected Text - prints the text you selected.

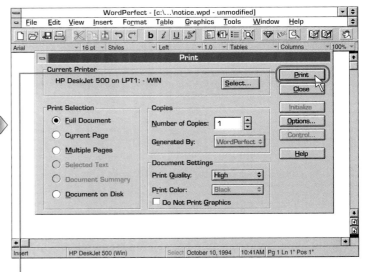

4 Move the mouse ▷ over **Print** and then press the left button.

73

PRINT AN ENVELOPE

You can use the Envelope feature to create and then print an envelope.

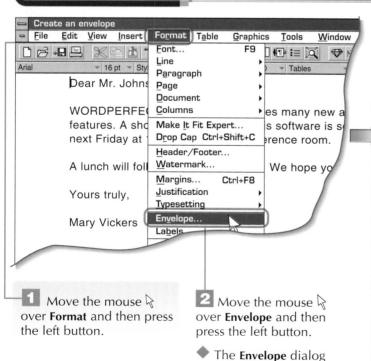

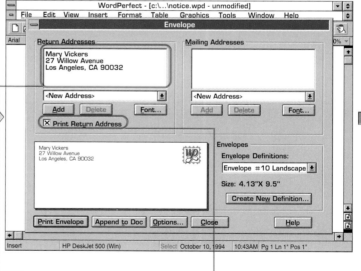

1 Move the mouse ⌖ over **Format** and then press the left button.

2 Move the mouse ⌖ over **Envelope** and then press the left button.

◆ The **Envelope** dialog box appears.

3 To enter a return address, move the mouse I over this area and then press the left button.

4 Type the return address. Press **Enter** after you type each line of text.

◆ If you do not want to print a return address, move the mouse ⌖ over **Print Return Address** and then press the left button (⊠ changes to ☐).

Getting
Started

Edit Your
Documents

Smart
Editing

Save and
Open Your
Documents

**Print Your
Documents**

Change Your
Document
Display

Using
Multiple
Documents

- Display Document Information
- Select a Printer
- Print a Document
- **Print an Envelope**
- Print Labels

You can use the Merge feature to create an envelope for each person on your mailing list.

Note: For more information, refer to page 194.

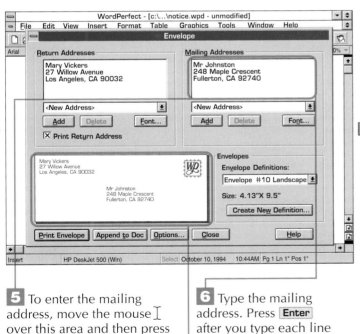

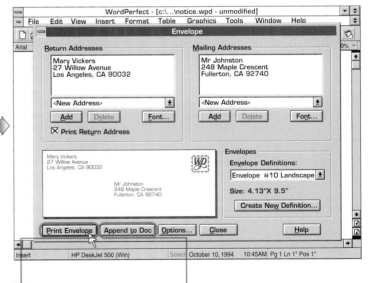

5 To enter the mailing address, move the mouse over this area and then press the left button.

Note: A mailing address automatically appears in this area if WordPerfect finds one in the current document.

6 Type the mailing address. Press **Enter** after you type each line of text.

◆ This area shows what your envelope will look like when printed.

7 To print the envelope, move the mouse over **Print Envelope** and then press the left button.

◆ To save and print the envelope with your document, move the mouse over **Append to Doc** and then press the left button. WordPerfect will attach the envelope to the end of your document.

PRINT LABELS

You can use the Labels feature to create shipping, file folder and diskette labels.

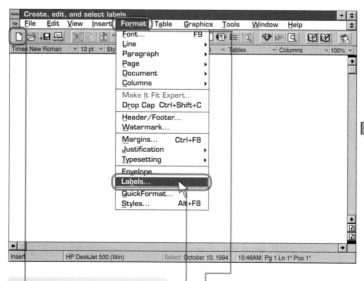

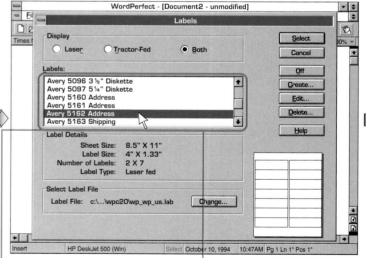

1 To create a new document, move the mouse ⬐ over 🗋 and then press the left button.

2 Move the mouse ⬐ over **Format** and then press the left button.

3 Move the mouse ⬐ over **Labels** and then press the left button.

◆ The **Labels** dialog box appears.

◆ This area displays the available labels.

Note: To view all of the available labels, use the scroll bar. For more information, refer to page 15.

4 Move the mouse ⬐ over the type of label you want to use and then press the left button.

Note: To select the correct label, refer to the label packaging.

Getting Started	Edit Your Documents	Smart Editing	Save and Open Your Documents	**Print Your Documents**	Change Your Document Display	Using Multiple Documents

- Display Document Information
- Select a Printer
- Print a Document
- Print an Envelope
- **Print Labels**

You can save and print labels as you would any document.

Note: For information on saving a document, refer to page 56. For information on printing a document, refer to page 72.

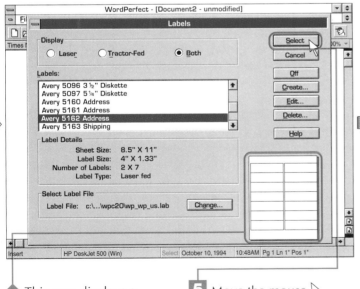

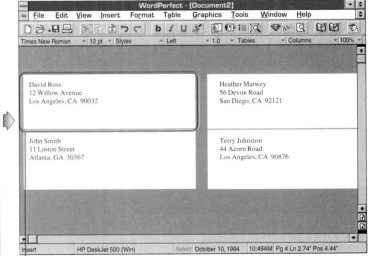

◆ This area displays a sample page of the label you selected.

5 Move the mouse over **Select** and then press the left button.

6 Type the text you want to appear on the label. To start a new line of text, press **Enter**.

7 When you finish typing the text for the label, press **Ctrl** + **Enter** to move to the next label.

8 Repeat steps **6** and **7** for each label you want to create.

verview

CHANGE YOUR DOCUMENT DISPLAY

Change Modes

Zoom In or Out

Display a WordPerfect Bar

Select a Toolbar

◇ In this chapter you will learn how to change the way your document appears on screen.

CHANGE MODES

WordPerfect offers three different ways to display your document. You can choose the mode that best suits your needs.

CHANGE THE DOCUMENT MODE

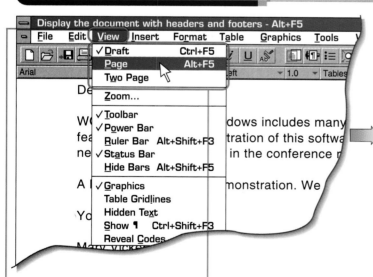

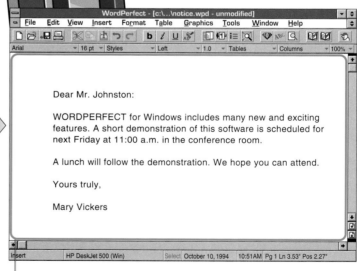

1 Move the mouse ⌖ over **View** and then press the left button.

2 Move the mouse ⌖ over the mode you want to use (example: **Page**) and then press the left button.

◆ Your document appears in the new mode.

| Getting Started | Edit Your Documents | Smart Editing | Save and Open Your Documents | Print Your Documents | **Change Your Document Display** | Using Multiple Documents |

• **Change Modes**
• Zoom In or Out
• Display a WordPerfect Bar
• Select a Toolbar

THE WORDPERFECT MODES

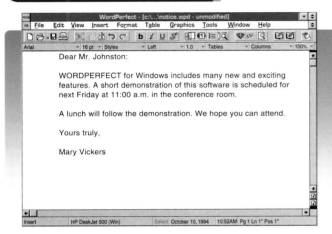

DRAFT MODE

◆ The **Draft** mode simplifies the page so you can quickly type and edit your document.

◆ This mode does not display top or bottom margins, headers, footers or page numbers.

PAGE MODE

◆ The **Page** mode displays your document exactly the way it will appear on a printed page.

◆ This mode displays top and bottom margins, headers, footers and page numbers.

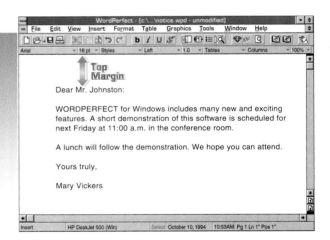

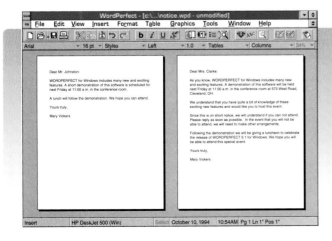

TWO PAGE MODE

◆ The **Two Page** mode displays two consecutive pages side by side.

◆ This mode displays top and bottom margins, headers, footers and page numbers.

ZOOM IN OR OUT

WordPerfect lets you enlarge or reduce the display of text on your screen. You can magnify the document to read small text or reduce the document to view more text.

ZOOM IN OR OUT

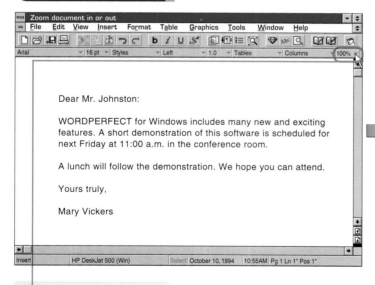

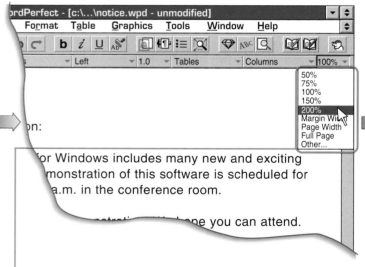

1 Move the mouse ⊠ over `100%` and then press the left button.

◆ In this example, the document is displayed in the Page mode. If your document is displayed in the Draft mode, the results of using the Zoom feature will look different.

Note: To change modes, refer to page 80.

2 Move the mouse ⊠ over the zoom setting you want to use (example: **200%**) and then press the left button.

*Note: The normal zoom setting is **100%**.*

Margin Width - displays text using the full width of the screen.

Page Width - displays the left and right edges of the page.

Full Page - displays the entire page.

Getting
Started

Edit Your
Documents

Smart
Editing

Save and
Open Your
Documents

Print Your
Documents

**Change Your
Document
Display**

Using
Multiple
Documents

- Change Modes
- **Zoom In or Out**
- Display a WordPerfect Bar
- Select a Toolbar

IMPORTANT!

You cannot use the Zoom feature if your document is displayed in the Two Page mode.

Note: For more information on the Two Page mode, refer to pages 80 to 81.

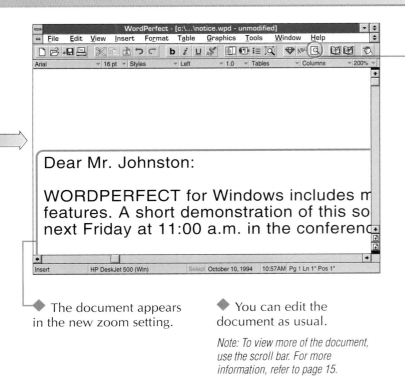

DISPLAY FULL PAGE

To quickly display an entire page, move the mouse ⟍ over 🔍 and then press the left button.

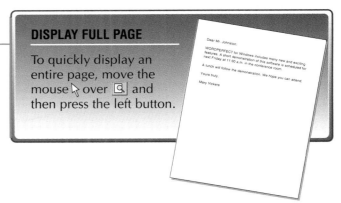

◆ The document appears in the new zoom setting.

◆ You can edit the document as usual.

Note: To view more of the document, use the scroll bar. For more information, refer to page 15.

DISPLAY A WORDPERFECT BAR

You can display one or all of the WordPerfect bars at any time.

DISPLAY A WORDPERFECT BAR

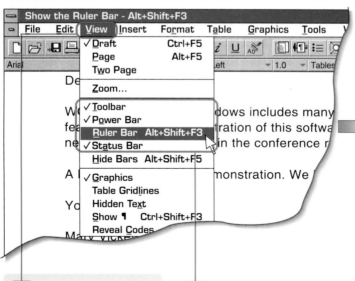

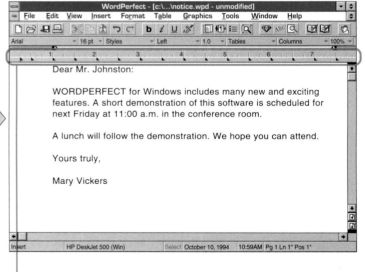

1 Move the mouse � over **View** and then press the left button.

2 Move the mouse � over the bar you want to display (example: **Ruler Bar**) and then press the left button.

Note: A check mark (✓) beside a bar name indicates the bar is currently displayed on your screen.

◆ The screen displays the bar you selected.

*Note: To remove a bar, repeat steps **1** and **2**.*

- Change Modes
- Zoom In or Out
- **Display a WordPerfect Bar**
- Select a Toolbar

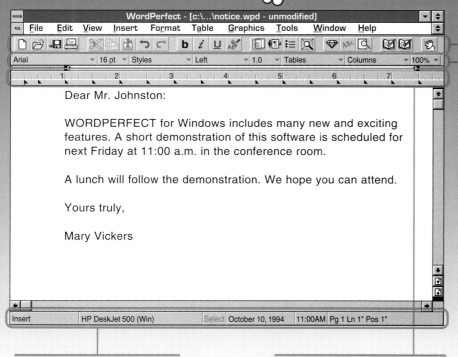

Toolbar

WordPerfect offers several Toolbars. Each Toolbar contains a series of buttons to help you quickly select commonly used commands.

Note: To display a different Toolbar, refer to page 86.

Power Bar

The Power Bar lets you quickly select formatting and layout features such as the size and alignment of text.

Status Bar

The Status Bar displays information about your document and the current date and time.

Ruler Bar

The Ruler Bar lets you change the margin and tab settings in your document.

SELECT A TOOLBAR

Each Toolbar contains buttons to help you quickly perform specific tasks. You can display one of these Toolbars at any time.

SELECT A TOOLBAR

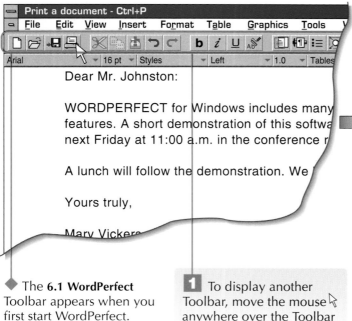

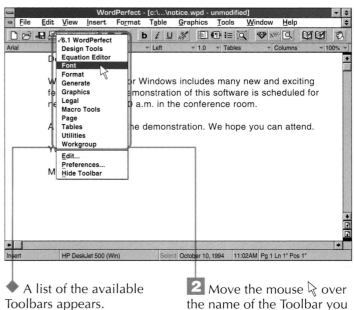

◆ The **6.1 WordPerfect** Toolbar appears when you first start WordPerfect.

1 To display another Toolbar, move the mouse over the Toolbar and then press the **right** button.

◆ A list of the available Toolbars appears.

2 Move the mouse over the name of the Toolbar you want to display (example: **Font**) and then press the left button.

INTRODUCTION TO WORDPERFECT

| Getting Started | Edit Your Documents | Smart Editing | Save and Open Your Documents | Print Your Documents | **Change Your Document Display** | Using Multiple Documents |

- Change Modes
- Zoom In or Out
- Display a WordPerfect Bar
- **Select a Toolbar**

WordPerfect offers several different Toolbars. Some examples include:

FONT

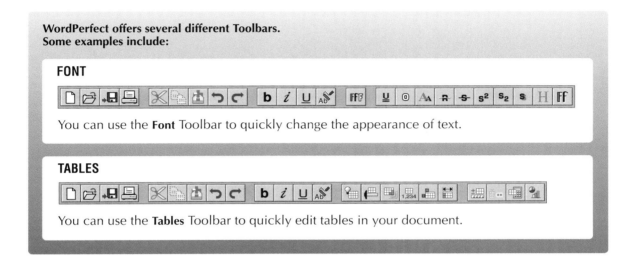

You can use the **Font** Toolbar to quickly change the appearance of text.

TABLES

You can use the **Tables** Toolbar to quickly edit tables in your document.

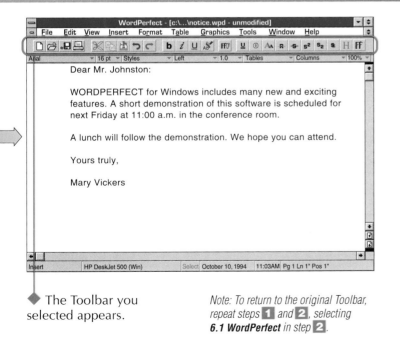

◆ The Toolbar you selected appears.

Note: To return to the original Toolbar, repeat steps 1 and 2, selecting **6.1 WordPerfect** *in step 2.*

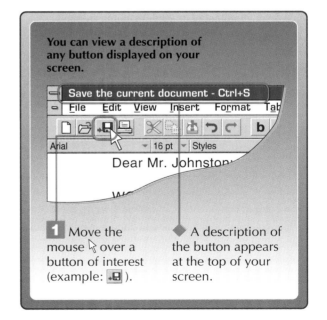

You can view a description of any button displayed on your screen.

1 Move the mouse over a button of interest (example:).

◆ A description of the button appears at the top of your screen.

verview

USING MULTIPLE DOCUMENTS

Create a New Document

Switch Between Documents

Arrange Open Documents

Copy or Move Text Between Documents

Close a Document

Maximize a Document

In this chapter you will learn how to create a new document and display more than one document at a time.

CREATE A NEW DOCUMENT   SWITCH BETWEEN DOCUMENTS

You can create a document to start a new letter, report or memo.

 CREATE A NEW DOCUMENT

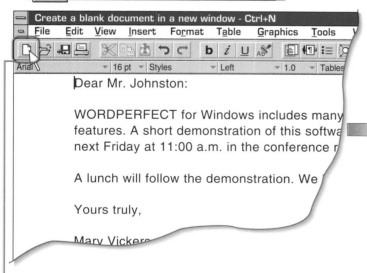

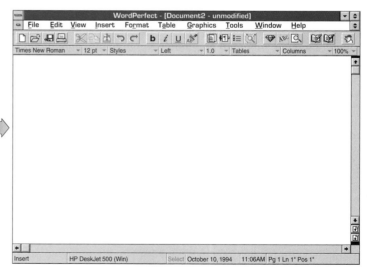

1 Move the mouse ⌖ over 🗋 and then press the left button.

◆ A new document appears.

Note: The previous document is now hidden behind the new document.

Getting Started	Edit Your Documents	Smart Editing	Save and Open Your Documents	Print Your Documents	Change Your Document Display	**Using Multiple Documents**

- **Create a New Document**
- **Switch Between Documents**
- Arrange Open Documents
- Copy or Move Text Between Documents
- Close a Document
- Maximize a Document

WordPerfect lets you have nine documents open at once. You can easily switch between all of these open documents.

SWITCH BETWEEN DOCUMENTS

1 To display a list of all your open documents, move the mouse ⌖ over **Window** and then press the left button.

2 Move the mouse ⌖ over the document you want to switch to and then press the left button.

◆ The document appears.

◆ WordPerfect displays the name of the document at the top of your screen.

ARRANGE OPEN DOCUMENTS

> If you have several documents open, some of them may be hidden from view. The Cascade command lets you display your open documents one on top of the other.

CASCADE OPEN DOCUMENTS

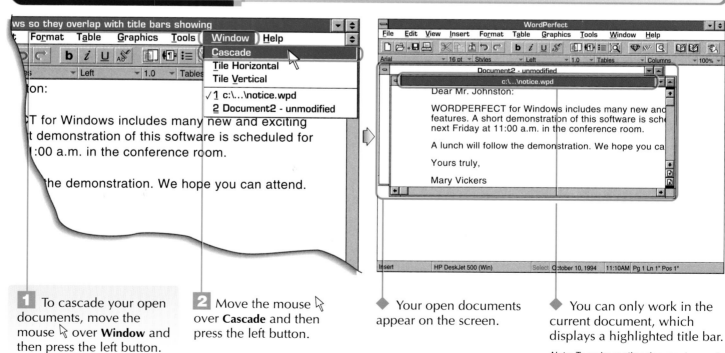

1 To cascade your open documents, move the mouse ⃗ over **Window** and then press the left button.

2 Move the mouse ⃗ over **Cascade** and then press the left button.

◆ Your open documents appear on the screen.

◆ You can only work in the current document, which displays a highlighted title bar.

Note: To make another document current, move the mouse ⃗ anywhere over the document and then press the left button.

Getting Started	Edit Your Documents	Smart Editing	Save and Open Your Documents	Print Your Documents	Change Your Document Display	Using Multiple Documents

- Create a New Document
- Switch Between Documents
- **Arrange Open Documents**
- Copy or Move Text Between Documents
- Close a Document
- Maximize a Document

> You can use the Tile command to view the contents of all of your open documents.

TILE OPEN DOCUMENTS

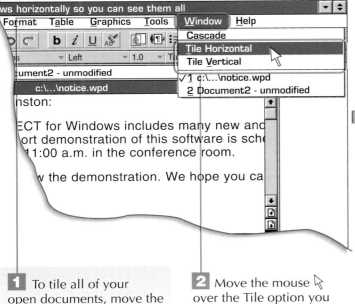

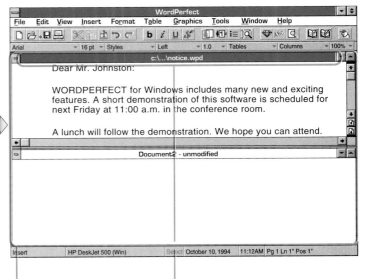

1 To tile all of your open documents, move the mouse over **Window** and then press the left button.

2 Move the mouse over the Tile option you want to use and then press the left button.

◆ You can now view the contents of all your open documents.

◆ You can only work in the current document, which displays a highlighted title bar.

Note: To make another document current, move the mouse anywhere over the document and then press the left button.

COPY OR MOVE TEXT BETWEEN DOCUMENTS

> Copying or moving text between documents saves you time when you are working in one document and want to use text from another.

COPY OR MOVE TEXT BETWEEN DOCUMENTS

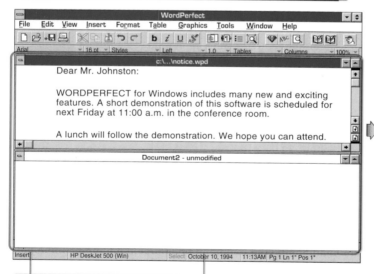

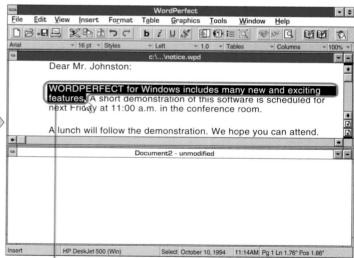

1 Open the documents you want to copy or move text between.

Note: To open a saved document, refer to page 62. To create a new document, refer to page 90.

2 Display the contents of the documents by using the Tile feature.

Note: To tile open documents, refer to page 93.

3 Select the text you want to copy or move to another document.

Note: To select text, refer to page 16.

4 Move the mouse I over the text you selected and I changes to ↘.

Getting
Started

Edit Your
Documents

Smart
Editing

Save and
Open Your
Documents

Print Your
Documents

Change Your
Document
Display

**Using
Multiple
Documents**

- Create a New Document
- Switch Between Documents
- Arrange Open Documents

- **Copy or Move Text Between Documents**
- Close a Document
- Maximize a Document

**The Copy and Move features both place text in a
new location, but they have one distinct difference.**

COPY TEXT

When you copy text, the
original text remains in
its place.

MOVE TEXT

When you move text, the
original text disappears.

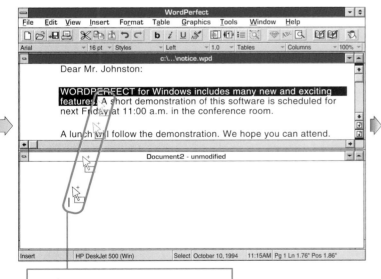

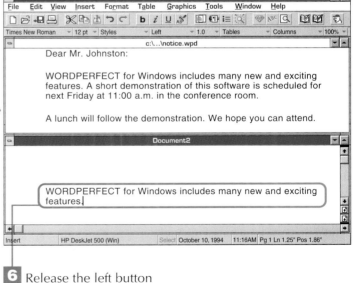

5 To copy the text, press and
hold down **Ctrl** and then press
and hold down the left button as
you drag the mouse where you
want to place the text.

◆ To move the text,
press and hold down the
left button as you drag
the mouse where you
want to place the text.

6 Release the left button
(and **Ctrl**) and the text
appears in the new
location.

CLOSE A DOCUMENT MAXIMIZE A DOCUMENT

When you finish working with a document, you can close it to remove the document from your screen.

CLOSE A DOCUMENT

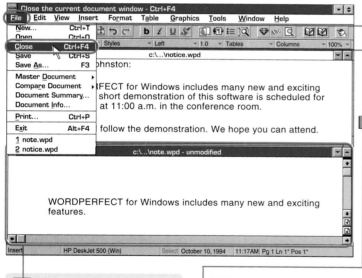

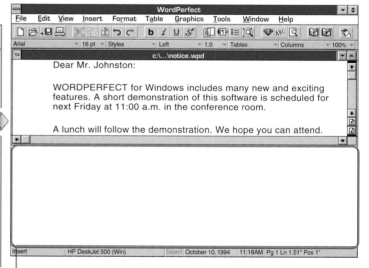

1 To select the document you want to close, move the mouse I over the document then press the left button.

2 To save the document before closing, refer to page 56.

3 Move the mouse over **File** and then press the left button.

4 Move the mouse over **Close** and then press the left button.

◆ WordPerfect removes the document from your screen.

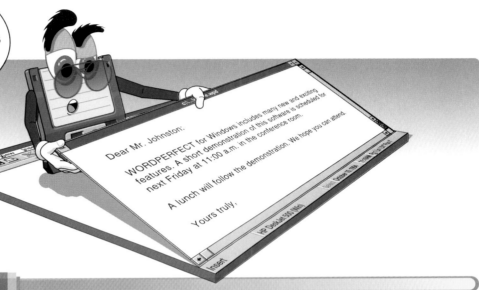

You can enlarge a document to fill your screen. This lets you view more of its contents.

MAXIMIZE A DOCUMENT

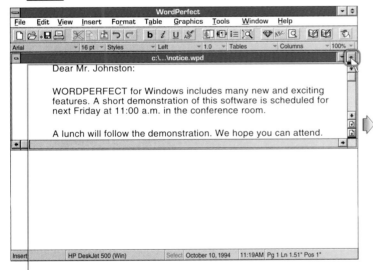

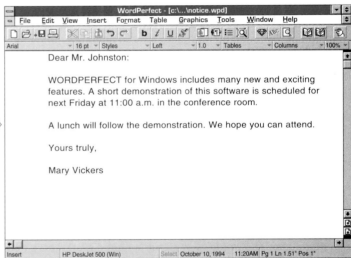

1 Move the mouse ▷ over ▲ in the document you want to maximize and then press the left button.

◆ The document enlarges to fill your screen.

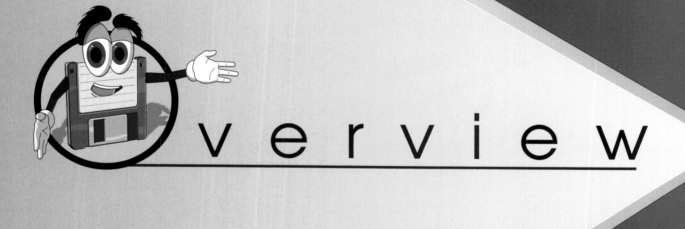
verview

FORMAT CHARACTERS

Bold, Italic and Underline

Change Fonts

Insert Special Characters

Using QuickFormat

◆ In this chapter you will learn how to change the appearance of text. You will also learn how to insert special characters into your document.

BOLD, ITALIC AND UNDERLINE

CHANGE FONTS

You can use the Bold, Italic and Underline features to emphasize important information.

Bold *Italic* <u>Underline</u>

BOLD, ITALIC AND UNDERLINE

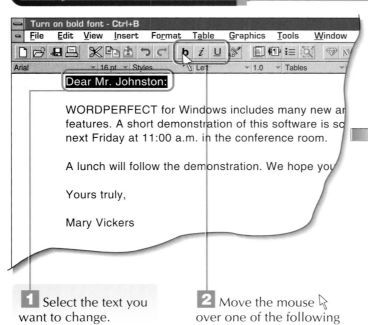

1 Select the text you want to change.

Note: To select text, refer to page 16.

2 Move the mouse  over one of the following options and then press the left button.

b	Bold text
i	Italicize text
U	Underline text

◆ The text you selected appears in the new style.

Note: In this example, the text appears in the bold style.

Remove Bold, Italic or Underline

Repeat steps **1** and **2**.

Format Characters	Format Paragraphs	Format Pages	Working With Tables	Using Graphics	Merge Documents	Time Saving Features

- **Bold, Italic and Underline**
- **Change Fonts**
- Insert Special Characters
- Using QuickFormat

> You can increase or decrease the size of text in your document. Increasing the size of text can make your document easier to read.

6 point
12 point
14 point
18 point
24 point

WordPerfect measures the size of text in points. There are approximately 72 points per inch.

CHANGE FONT SIZE

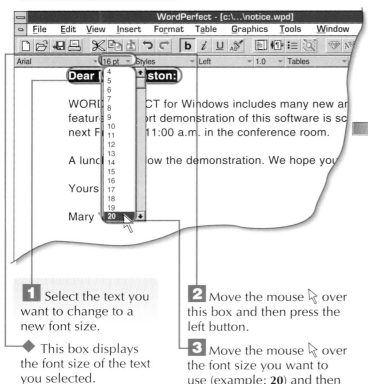

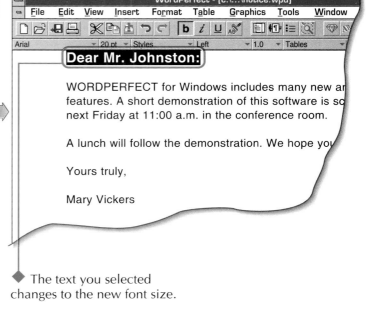

1 Select the text you want to change to a new font size.

◆ This box displays the font size of the text you selected.

2 Move the mouse ⌖ over this box and then press the left button.

3 Move the mouse ⌖ over the font size you want to use (example: **20**) and then press the left button.

◆ The text you selected changes to the new font size.

101

CHANGE FONTS

You can change the design of characters in your document to emphasize headings and make text easier to read.

CHANGE FONT FACE

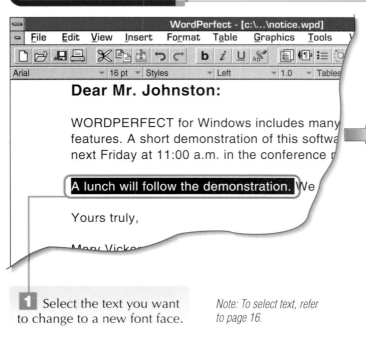

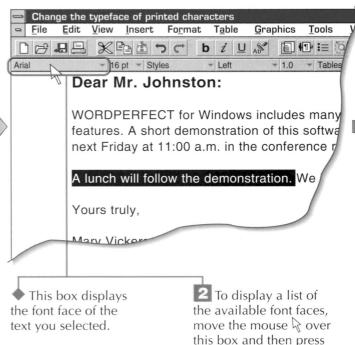

1 Select the text you want to change to a new font face.

Note: To select text, refer to page 16.

◆ This box displays the font face of the text you selected.

2 To display a list of the available font faces, move the mouse ⟲ over this box and then press the left button.

Format Characters	Format Paragraphs	Format Pages	Working With Tables	Using Graphics	Merge Documents	Time Saving Features

- Bold, Italic and Underline
- **Change Fonts**
- Insert Special Characters
- Using QuickFormat

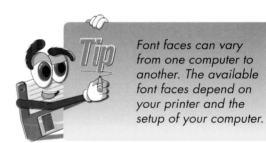

Font faces can vary from one computer to another. The available font faces depend on your printer and the setup of your computer.

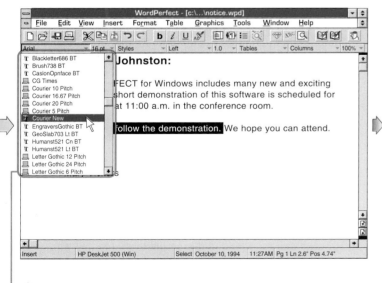

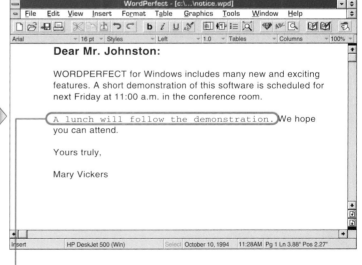

◆ A list of the available font faces appears.

3 Move the mouse ⬡ over the font face you want to use (example: **Courier New**) and then press the left button.

Note: To view all of the available font faces, use the scroll bar. For more information, refer to page 15.

◆ The text you selected changes to the new font face.

Note: To deselect text, move the mouse I outside the selected area and then press the left button.

◆ To select a different font face, repeat steps **1** to **3**.

CHANGE FONTS

You can use the Font dialog box to change the design and size of characters in your document at the same time. This lets you turn a dull, lifeless letter into an interesting, attractive document.

CHANGE FONTS

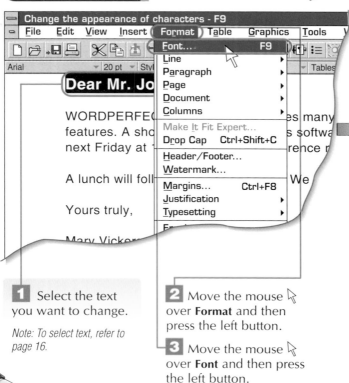

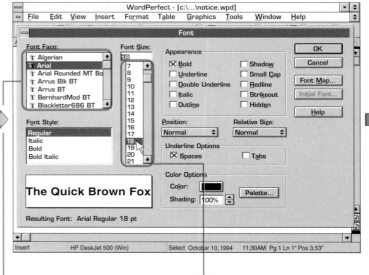

1 Select the text you want to change.

Note: To select text, refer to page 16.

2 Move the mouse over **Format** and then press the left button.

3 Move the mouse over **Font** and then press the left button.

◆ The **Font** dialog box appears.

4 Move the mouse over the font face you want to use (example: **Arial**) and then press the left button.

5 Move the mouse over the font size you want to use (example: **18**) and then press the left button.

Note: To view more font faces or sizes, use the scroll bar. For more information, refer to page 15.

Format **Characters**	Format Paragraphs	Format Pages	Working With Tables	Using Graphics	Merge Documents	Time Saving Features

- Bold, Italic and Underline
- **Change Fonts**
- Insert Special Characters
- Using QuickFormat

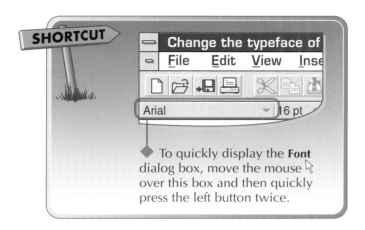

SHORTCUT

◆ To quickly display the **Font** dialog box, move the mouse over this box and then quickly press the left button twice.

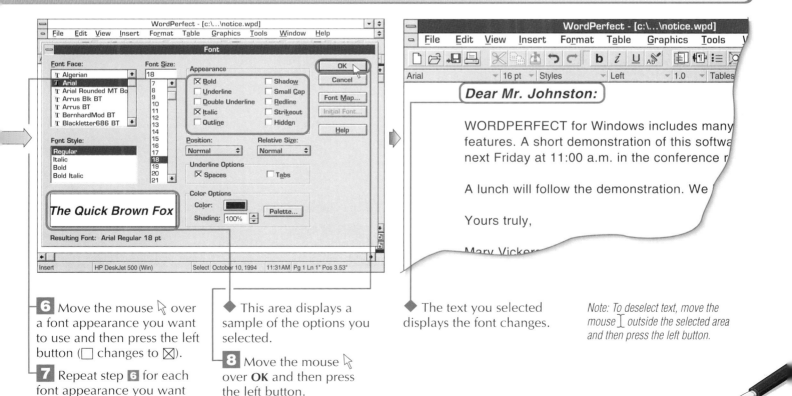

◢ **6** Move the mouse over a font appearance you want to use and then press the left button (☐ changes to ☒).

◢ **7** Repeat step **6** for each font appearance you want to use.

◆ This area displays a sample of the options you selected.

8 Move the mouse over **OK** and then press the left button.

◆ The text you selected displays the font changes.

Note: To deselect text, move the mouse outside the selected area and then press the left button.

CHANGE FONTS

You can change WordPerfect's initial font. This is useful if you want all of your future documents to start with a specific font.

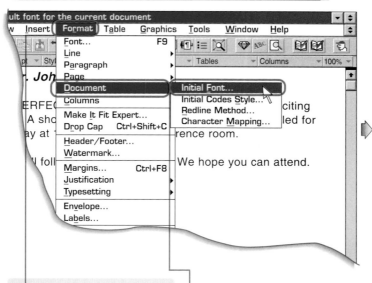

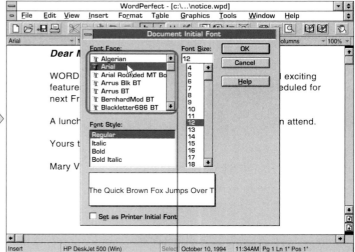

1 Move the mouse over **Format** and then press the left button.

2 Move the mouse over **Document** and then press the left button.

3 Move the mouse over **Initial Font** and then press the left button.

◆ The **Document Initial Font** dialog box appears.

4 Move the mouse over the font face you want to use (example: **Arial**) and then press the left button.

Note: To view all of the available font faces, use the scroll bar. For more information, refer to page 15.

106

Format Characters	Format Paragraphs	Format Pages	Working With Tables	Using Graphics	Merge Documents	Time Saving Features

- Bold, Italic and Underline
- **Change Fonts**
- Insert Special Characters
- Using QuickFormat

*Changing the initial font will **not** affect documents you have already created. To change the font of text in existing documents, refer to pages 101 to 105.*

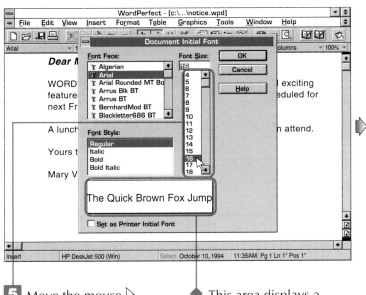

5 Move the mouse ▷ over the font size you want to use (example: **16**) and then press the left button.

◆ This area displays a sample of the font you selected.

6 To use this font in all of your future documents, move the mouse ▷ over this option and then press the left button (☐ changes to ☒).

7 Move the mouse ▷ over **OK** and then press the left button.

INSERT SPECIAL CHARACTERS

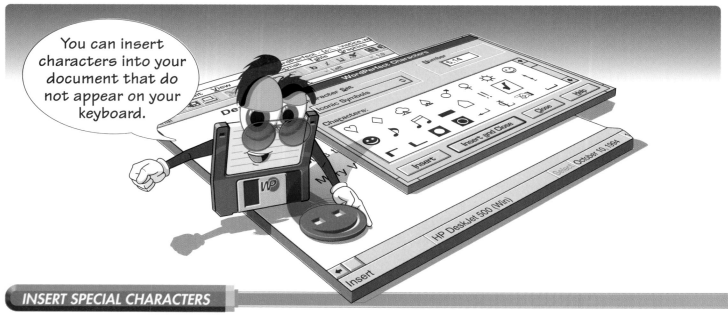

> You can insert characters into your document that do not appear on your keyboard.

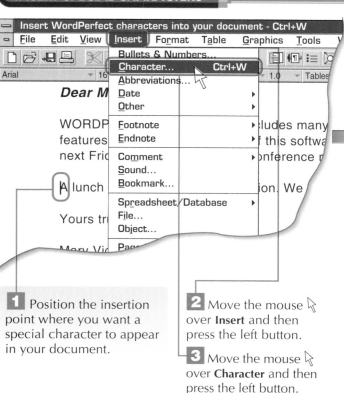

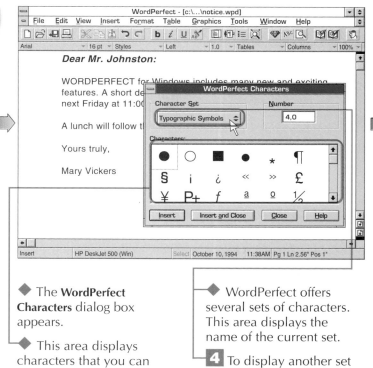

1 Position the insertion point where you want a special character to appear in your document.

2 Move the mouse over **Insert** and then press the left button.

3 Move the mouse over **Character** and then press the left button.

◆ The **WordPerfect Characters** dialog box appears.

◆ This area displays characters that you can insert into your document.

Note: To view more characters, use the scroll bar. For more information, refer to page 15.

◆ WordPerfect offers several sets of characters. This area displays the name of the current set.

4 To display another set of characters, move the mouse over this box and then press and hold down the left button.

| Format Characters | Format Paragraphs | Format Pages | Working With Tables | Using Graphics | Merge Documents | Time Saving Features |

- Bold, Italic and Underline
- Change Fonts
- **Insert Special Characters**
- Using QuickFormat

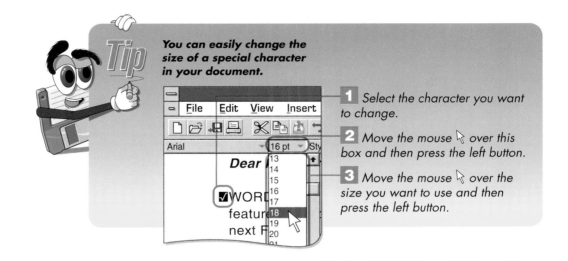

You can easily change the size of a special character in your document.

1 Select the character you want to change.

2 Move the mouse ⬚ over this box and then press the left button.

3 Move the mouse ⬚ over the size you want to use and then press the left button.

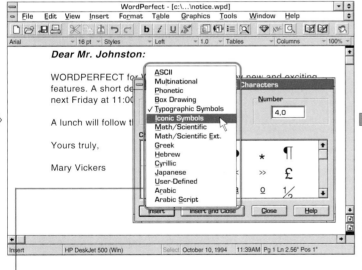

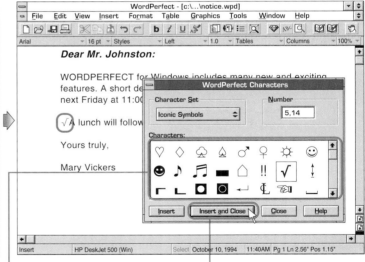

5 Still holding down the button, move the mouse ⬚ over the character set you want to view. Then release the button.

◆ The characters in the new set appear.

6 Move the mouse ⬚ over the character you want to place in your document and then press the left button.

7 Move the mouse ⬚ over **Insert and Close** and then press the left button.

◆ The character appears in your document.

USING QUICKFORMAT

The QuickFormat feature lets you easily copy the appearance of text in your document. This is useful if you want different areas of text to look the same.

 USING QUICKFORMAT

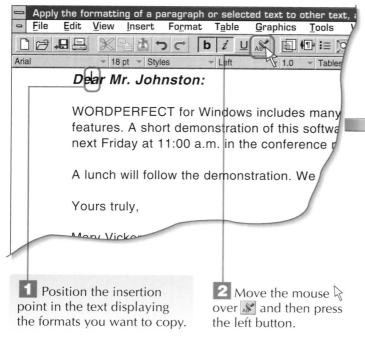

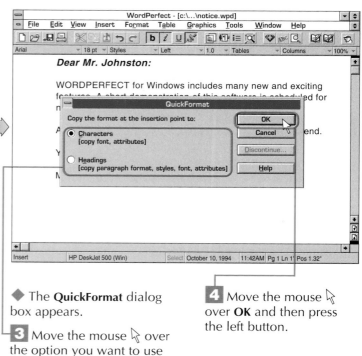

1 Position the insertion point in the text displaying the formats you want to copy.

2 Move the mouse ⬚ over 🖌 and then press the left button.

◆ The **QuickFormat** dialog box appears.

3 Move the mouse ⬚ over the option you want to use and then press the left button (○ changes to ◉).

4 Move the mouse ⬚ over **OK** and then press the left button.

| Format **Characters** | Format Paragraphs | Format Pages | Working With Tables | Using Graphics | Merge Documents | Time Saving Features |

- Bold, Italic and Underline
- Change Fonts
- Insert Special Characters
- **Using QuickFormat**

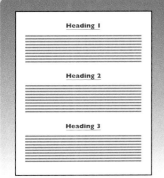

Headings

◆ This option is useful when you want all of the headings in your document to look the same.

◆ If you change the formats of one heading, WordPerfect will automatically change the formats of all the others.

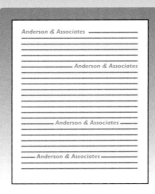

Characters

◆ This option is useful when you want to emphasize specific words or phrases in your document, such as a company name.

◆ If you change the formats of a word or phrase, WordPerfect will **not** automatically change the formats of all the others.

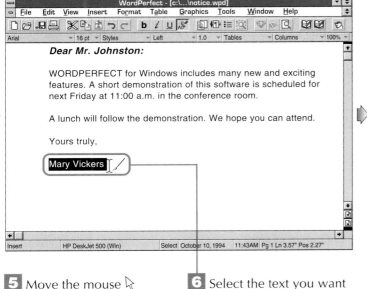

5 Move the mouse ↖ over your document and ↖ changes to I⁄.

6 Select the text you want to display the formats.

◆ When you release the left button, the text you selected displays the new formats.

7 Repeat step **6** until you have selected all the text you want to display the formats.

8 When you finish copying the formats, move the mouse ↖ over 🖉 and then press the left button.

verview

FORMAT PARAGRAPHS

Justify Text

Change Line Spacing

Change Tab Settings

Indent a Paragraph

Add Bullets and Numbers

Add Borders and Shading

◇ In this chapter you will learn how to change the appearance of paragraphs in your document.

JUSTIFY TEXT

You can enhance the appearance of your document by justifying text in different ways. WordPerfect offers several justification options.

- Right
- Center
- Left
- Full
- All

JUSTIFY TEXT

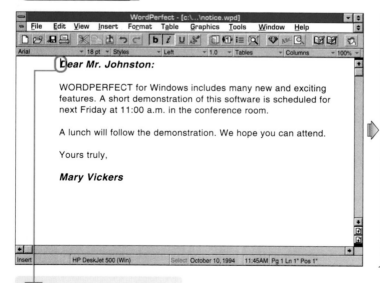

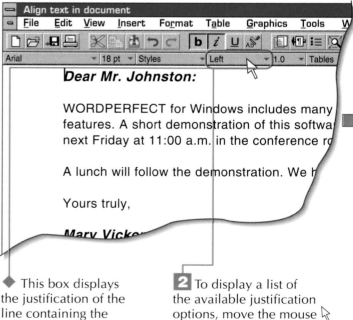

1 Position the insertion point where you want the new justification to begin.

Note: To change the justification of a section of text, select the text you want to change. To select text, refer to page 16.

◆ This box displays the justification of the line containing the insertion point.

2 To display a list of the available justification options, move the mouse over this box and then press the left button.

Format Characters	**Format Paragraphs**	Format Pages	Working With Tables	Using Graphics	Merge Documents	Time Saving Features

- **Justify Text**
- Change Line Spacing
- Change Tab Settings
- Indent a Paragraph
- Add Bullets and Numbers
- Add Borders and Shading

Tip

You can also vertically center text on a page.

Note: For more information, refer to page 136.

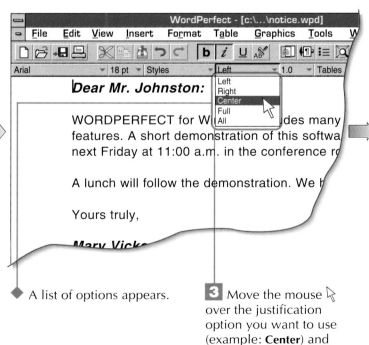

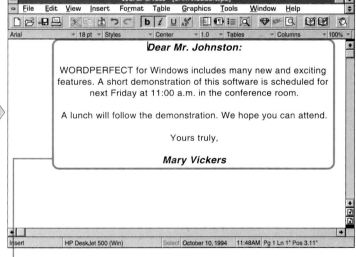

◆ A list of options appears.

3 Move the mouse over the justification option you want to use (example: **Center**) and then press the left button.

◆ The paragraph containing the insertion point and all text that follows display the new justification.

*Note: To return to the original justification, repeat steps **1** to **3**, selecting **Left** in step **3**.*

CHANGE LINE SPACING

> You can make your document easier to read by changing the amount of space between the lines of text.

1.0 line spacing
This is the initial (or default) setting.

1.5 line spacing

2.0 line spacing

CHANGE LINE SPACING

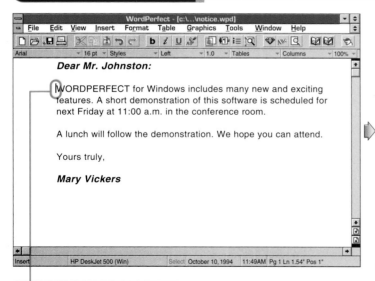

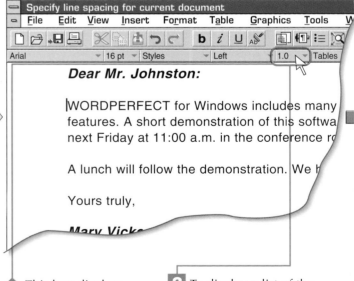

1 Position the insertion point where you want the new line spacing to begin.

Note: To change the line spacing of a section of text, select the text you want to change. To select text, refer to page 16.

◆ This box displays the line spacing of the paragraph containing the insertion point.

2 To display a list of the available line spacing options, move the mouse ⬡ over this box and then press the left button.

Format Characters	**Format Paragraphs**	Format Pages	Working With Tables	Using Graphics	Merge Documents	Time Saving Features

- Justify Text
- **Change Line Spacing**
- Change Tab Settings
- Indent a Paragraph
- Add Bullets and Numbers
- Add Borders and Shading

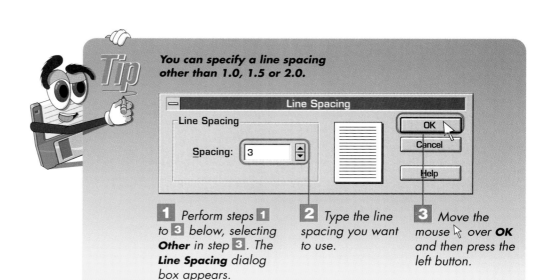

You can specify a line spacing other than 1.0, 1.5 or 2.0.

1 Perform steps **1** to **3** below, selecting **Other** in step **3**. The **Line Spacing** dialog box appears.

2 Type the line spacing you want to use.

3 Move the mouse over **OK** and then press the left button.

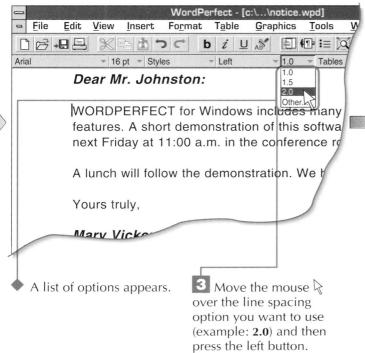

◆ A list of options appears.

3 Move the mouse over the line spacing option you want to use (example: **2.0**) and then press the left button.

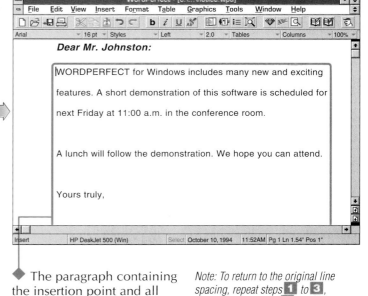

◆ The paragraph containing the insertion point and all text that follows display the new line spacing.

*Note: To return to the original line spacing, repeat steps **1** to **3**, selecting **1.0** in step **3**.*

CHANGE TAB SETTINGS

You can use tabs to line up columns of information in your document.

Make sure you use tabs rather than spaces to line up columns of text. This will ensure your document prints correctly.

◆ In this example, spaces were used to line up columns.

◆ In this example, tabs were used to line up columns.

DELETE A TAB

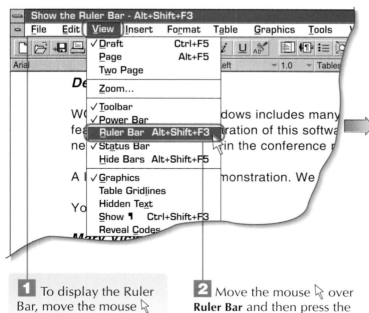

1 To display the Ruler Bar, move the mouse ⍟ over **View** and then press the left button.

2 Move the mouse ⍟ over **Ruler Bar** and then press the left button.

*Note: To hide the Ruler Bar, repeat steps **1** and **2**.*

◆ The Ruler Bar appears displaying the current tab locations. WordPerfect initially sets a left tab (▲) at every half inch.

3 Position the insertion point where you want the new tab settings to begin.

Format Characters	**Format Paragraphs**	Format Pages	Working With Tables	Using Graphics	Merge Documents	Time Saving Features

- Justify Text
- Change Line Spacing
- **Change Tab Settings**
- Indent a Paragraph
- Add Bullets and Numbers
- Add Borders and Shading

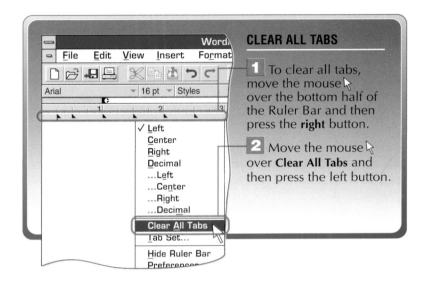

CLEAR ALL TABS

1 To clear all tabs, move the mouse over the bottom half of the Ruler Bar and then press the **right** button.

2 Move the mouse over **Clear All Tabs** and then press the left button.

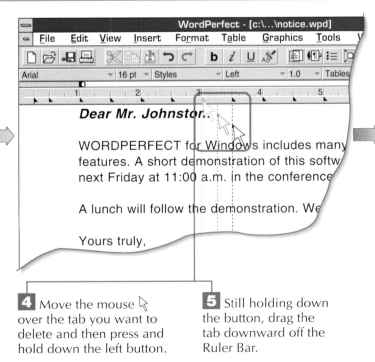

4 Move the mouse over the tab you want to delete and then press and hold down the left button.

5 Still holding down the button, drag the tab downward off the Ruler Bar.

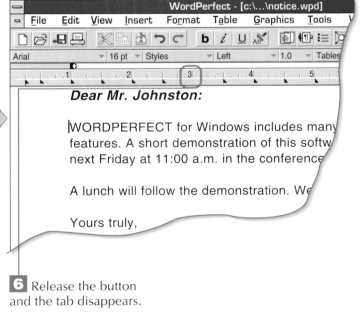

6 Release the button and the tab disappears.

CHANGE TAB SETTINGS

WordPerfect offers four types of tabs to help you line up text in your document.

Left tab
Right tab
Center tab
123.45 (Decimal tab)

Tab position

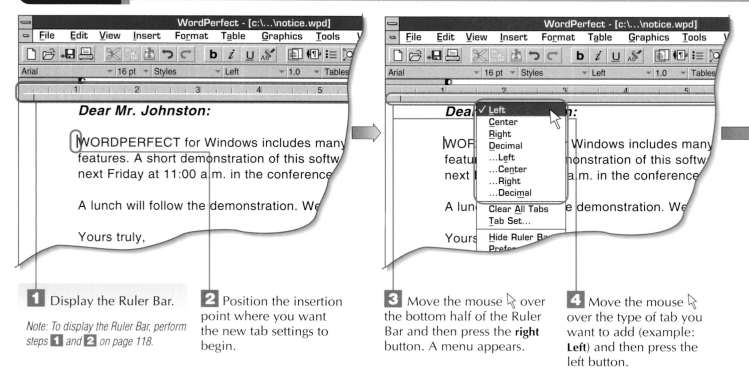

1 Display the Ruler Bar.

Note: To display the Ruler Bar, perform steps 1 and 2 on page 118.

2 Position the insertion point where you want the new tab settings to begin.

3 Move the mouse ⌖ over the bottom half of the Ruler Bar and then press the **right** button. A menu appears.

4 Move the mouse ⌖ over the type of tab you want to add (example: **Left**) and then press the left button.

Format Characters	**Format Paragraphs**	Format Pages	Working With Tables	Using Graphics	Merge Documents	Time Saving Features

- Justify Text
- Change Line Spacing
- **Change Tab Settings**
- Indent a Paragraph
- Add Bullets and Numbers
- Add Borders and Shading

You can insert a row of dots before a tab to help lead the eye from one column of information to another. This is useful if you want to create a Table of Contents.

. . . . **Left tab**
. . . **Right tab**
. . . .**Center tab**
. . . .**123.45** (Decimal tab)

Tab position

Tab ⇥ **USING TABS**

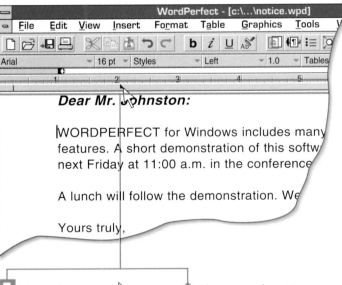

5 Move the mouse � over the position on the Ruler Bar where you want to add the tab and then press the left button.

◆ The new tab setting appears on the Ruler Bar.

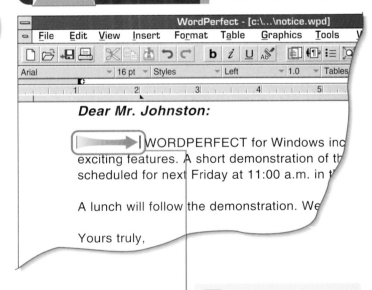

After you have set tabs, you can use them to quickly move the insertion point across your screen.

1 Position the insertion point at the beginning of the line you want to move across.

2 Press **Tab** and the insertion point and all text that follows move to the first tab stop.

INDENT A PARAGRAPH

Indent

Hanging Indent

Double Indent

You can use the Indent feature to emphasize paragraphs in your document.

INDENT A PARAGRAPH

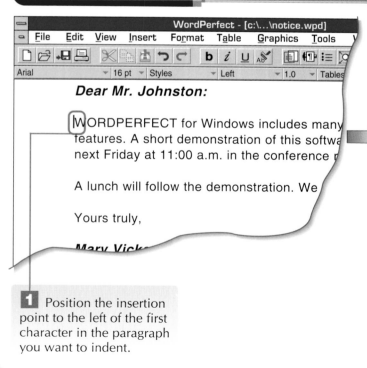

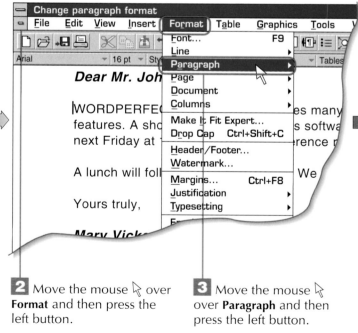

1 Position the insertion point to the left of the first character in the paragraph you want to indent.

2 Move the mouse over **Format** and then press the left button.

3 Move the mouse over **Paragraph** and then press the left button.

Format Characters	**Format Paragraphs**	Format Pages	Working With Tables	Using Graphics	Merge Documents	Time Saving Features

- Justify Text
- Change Line Spacing
- Change Tab Settings

- **Indent a Paragraph**
- Add Bullets and Numbers
- Add Borders and Shading

When you indent a paragraph, the paragraph moves to the first tab setting. To change the distance the paragraph moves, change the tab settings.

Note: For more information on changing tab settings, refer to pages 118 to 121.

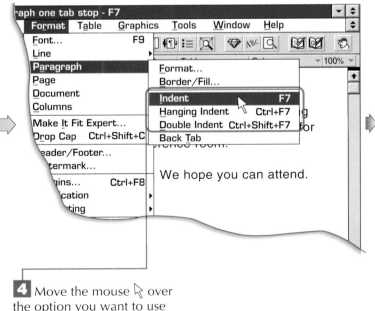

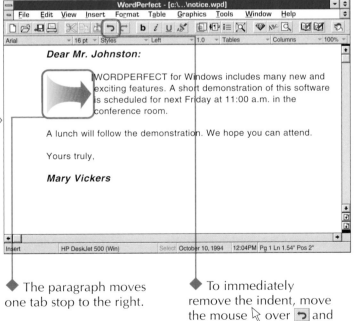

4 Move the mouse ⬚ over the option you want to use (example: **Indent**) and then press the left button.

◆ The paragraph moves one tab stop to the right.

◆ To immediately remove the indent, move the mouse ⬚ over � and then press the left button.

123

ADD BULLETS AND NUMBERS

> You can separate items in a list by beginning each item with a bullet or number.

◆ **Numbers** are useful for items in a specific order, such as a recipe.

◆ **Bullets** are useful for items in no particular order, such as a list of goals.

ADD BULLETS AND NUMBERS

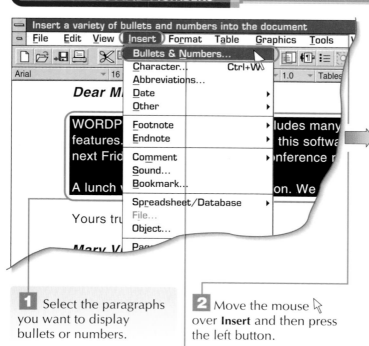

1 Select the paragraphs you want to display bullets or numbers.

2 Move the mouse ☐ over **Insert** and then press the left button.

3 Move the mouse ☐ over **Bullets & Numbers** and then press the left button.

◆ The **Bullets & Numbers** dialog box appears.

4 Move the mouse ☐ over the style you want to use (example: **Numbers**) and then press the left button.

Format Characters	**Format Paragraphs**	Format Pages	Working With Tables	Using Graphics	Merge Documents	Time Saving Features

- Justify Text
- Change Line Spacing
- Change Tab Settings
- Indent a Paragraph
- **Add Bullets and Numbers**
- Add Borders and Shading

Tip

If you add a new item to your list, WordPerfect will automatically renumber the items.

This only works if you selected **New Bullet or Number on ENTER** in step **5** below.

1	Word Processors
	Spreadsheets
2	Databases
3	Desktop Publishing

1	Word Processors
2	Spreadsheets
3	Databases
4	Desktop Publishing

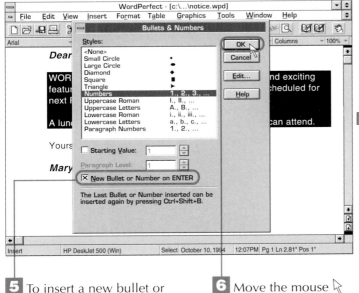

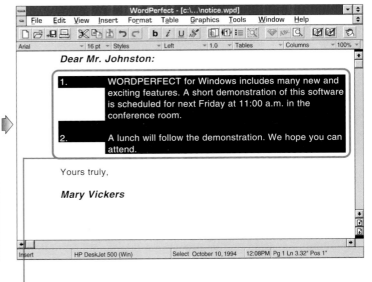

5 To insert a new bullet or number every time you press **Enter**, move the mouse ⌖ over this option and then press the left button (☐ changes to ☒).

6 Move the mouse ⌖ over **OK** and then press the left button.

◆ The bullets or numbers appear in your document.

Note: To remove the bullets or numbers, repeat steps **1** *to* **4**, *selecting* **<None>** *in step* **4**. *Then perform step* **6**.

125

ADD BORDERS AND SHADING

You can add borders and shading to draw attention to important information in your document.

ADD BORDERS AND SHADING

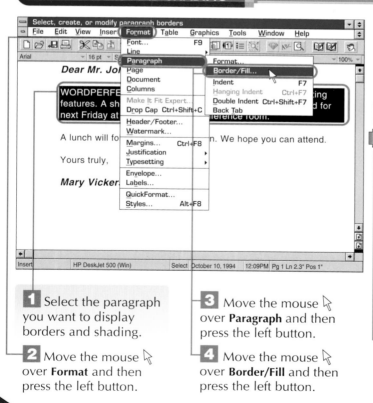

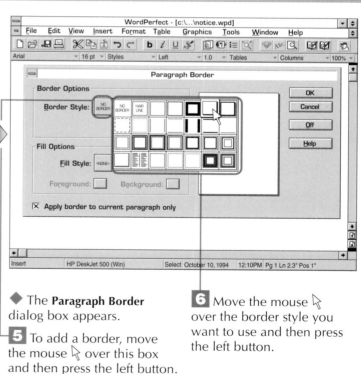

1 Select the paragraph you want to display borders and shading.

2 Move the mouse over **Format** and then press the left button.

3 Move the mouse over **Paragraph** and then press the left button.

4 Move the mouse over **Border/Fill** and then press the left button.

◆ The **Paragraph Border** dialog box appears.

5 To add a border, move the mouse over this box and then press the left button.

6 Move the mouse over the border style you want to use and then press the left button.

Format Characters	**Format Paragraphs**	Format Pages	Working With Tables	Using Graphics	Merge Documents	Time Saving Features

- Justify Text
- Change Line Spacing
- Change Tab Settings
- Indent a Paragraph
- Add Bullets and Numbers
- **Add Borders and Shading**

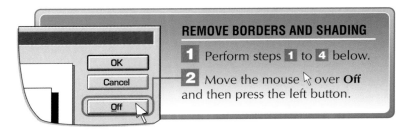

REMOVE BORDERS AND SHADING

1 Perform steps **1** to **4** below.

2 Move the mouse � over **Off** and then press the left button.

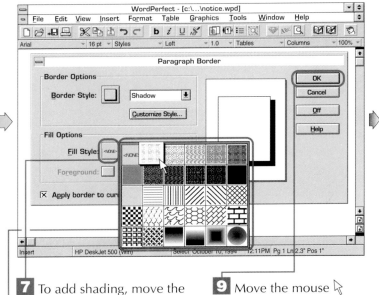

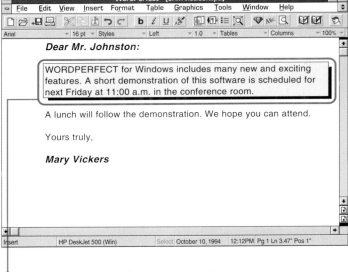

7 To add shading, move the mouse � over this box and then press the left button.

8 Move the mouse � over the fill style you want to use and then press the left button.

9 Move the mouse � over **OK** and then press the left button.

◆ The paragraph displays the border and shading styles you selected.

Note: To deselect a paragraph, move the mouse I outside the selected area and then press the left button.

127

FORMAT PAGES

Insert a Page Break

Change Margins

Center a Page

Add Page Numbers

Change Paper Size

Make Text Fit

Add Headers or Footers

Suppress a Header or Footer

Add Footnotes

Create Columns

In this chapter you will learn how to change the look of entire pages in your document. You will also learn how to add information to your document.

INSERT A PAGE BREAK

If you want to start a new page at a specific place in your document, you can insert a page break. A page break defines where one page ends and another begins.

A page break you inserted.

A page break WordPerfect inserted.

When you fill an entire page with text, WordPerfect automatically starts a new one by inserting a page break.

INSERT A PAGE BREAK

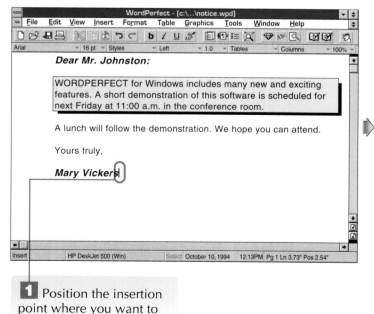

1 Position the insertion point where you want to start a new page.

2 Move the mouse over **Insert** and then press the left button.

3 Move the mouse over **Page Break** and then press the left button.

DELETE A PAGE BREAK YOU INSERTED

1 Position the insertion point after the last character on the page before the page break line.

2 Press Delete .

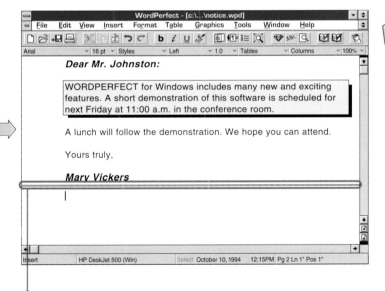

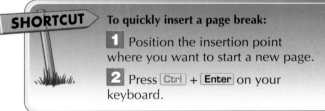

SHORTCUT

To quickly insert a page break:

1 Position the insertion point where you want to start a new page.

2 Press Ctrl + Enter on your keyboard.

◆ A double line appears across your screen. This line defines where one page ends and another begins.

Note: This line will not appear when you print your document.

CHANGE MARGINS

WordPerfect automatically sets the left and right margins in your document at one inch. You can change these settings to shorten or lengthen your document.

A margin is the amount of space between text and an edge of your paper.

CHANGE LEFT AND RIGHT MARGINS

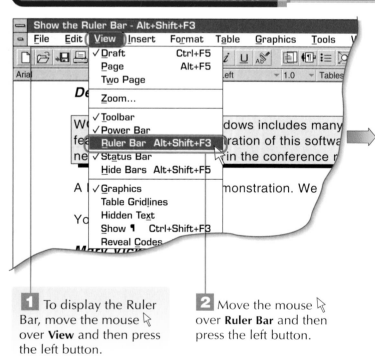

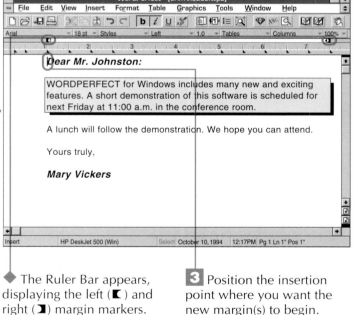

1 To display the Ruler Bar, move the mouse ⌖ over **View** and then press the left button.

2 Move the mouse ⌖ over **Ruler Bar** and then press the left button.

◆ The Ruler Bar appears, displaying the left (◀) and right (▶) margin markers.

3 Position the insertion point where you want the new margin(s) to begin.

Note: To change the margin(s) of a section of text, you must first select the text. To select text, refer to page 16.

132

Format Characters	Format Paragraphs	**Format Pages**	Working With Tables	Using Graphics	Merge Documents	Time Saving Features

- Insert a Page Break
- **Change Margins**
- Center a Page
- Add Page Numbers
- Change Paper Size

- Make Text Fit
- Add Headers or Footers
- Suppress a Header or Footer
- Add Footnotes
- Create Columns

MARGIN MARKERS

The Ruler Bar displays the margin markers. These markers indicate the position of the left and right margins. You can move these markers to change the margin settings.

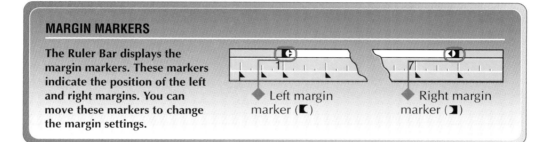

◆ Left margin marker (◤)   ◆ Right margin marker (◥)

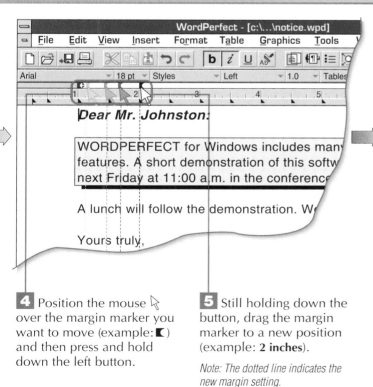

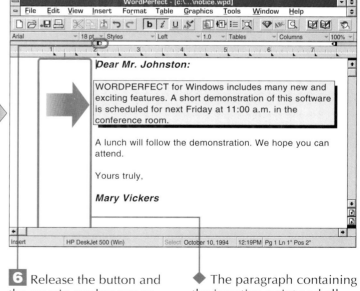

4 Position the mouse ▷ over the margin marker you want to move (example: ◤) and then press and hold down the left button.

5 Still holding down the button, drag the margin marker to a new position (example: **2 inches**).

Note: The dotted line indicates the new margin setting.

6 Release the button and the margin marker moves to the new position.

◆ The paragraph containing the insertion point and all text that follows display the new margin(s).

*Note: To hide the Ruler Bar, repeat steps **1** and **2**.*

CHANGE MARGINS

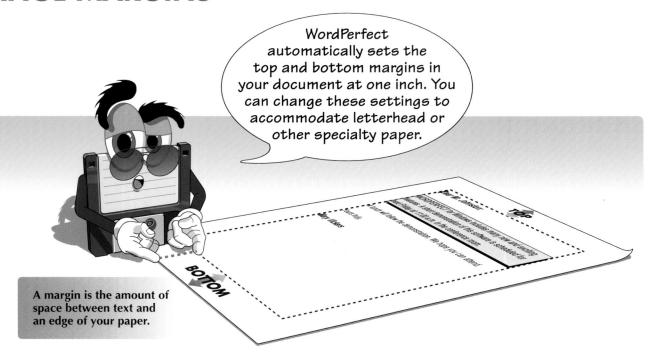

WordPerfect automatically sets the top and bottom margins in your document at one inch. You can change these settings to accommodate letterhead or other specialty paper.

A margin is the amount of space between text and an edge of your paper.

CHANGE TOP AND BOTTOM MARGINS

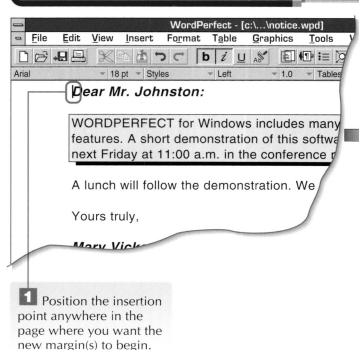

1 Position the insertion point anywhere in the page where you want the new margin(s) to begin.

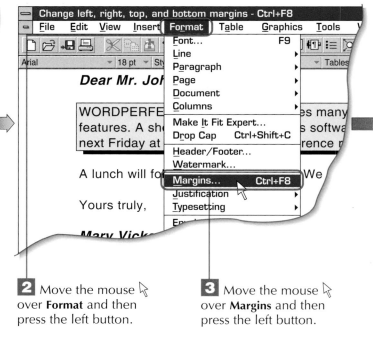

2 Move the mouse over **Format** and then press the left button.

3 Move the mouse over **Margins** and then press the left button.

Format Characters	Format Paragraphs	**Format Pages**	Working With Tables	Using Graphics	Merge Documents	Time Saving Features

- Insert a Page Break
- **Change Margins**
- Center a Page
- Add Page Numbers
- Change Paper Size

- Make Text Fit
- Add Headers or Footers
- Suppress a Header or Footer
- Add Footnotes
- Create Columns

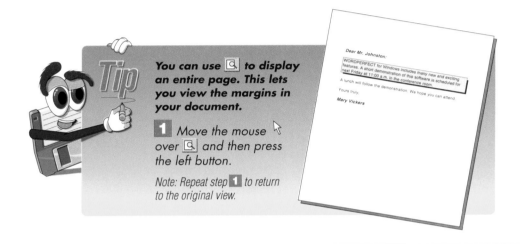

You can use 🔍 *to display an entire page. This lets you view the margins in your document.*

1 Move the mouse over 🔍 and then press the left button.

Note: Repeat step **1** *to return to the original view.*

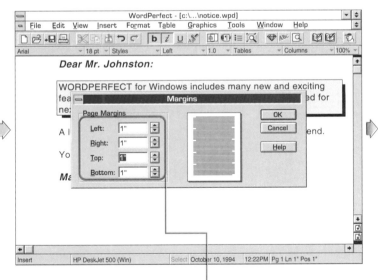

◆ The **Margins** dialog box appears.

Note: You can use this dialog box to change the left, right, top and bottom margins.

4 Press **Tab** until you highlight the number beside the margin you want to change (example: **Top**).

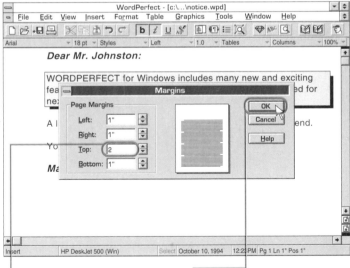

5 Type the new margin in inches (example: **2**).

Note: Repeat steps **4** *and* **5** *for each margin you want to change.*

6 Move the mouse ⌖ over **OK** and then press the left button.

◆ The page containing the insertion point and all pages that follow change to the new margin(s).

CENTER A PAGE

You can vertically center text on a page. This is useful for creating title pages or short memos.

CENTER A PAGE

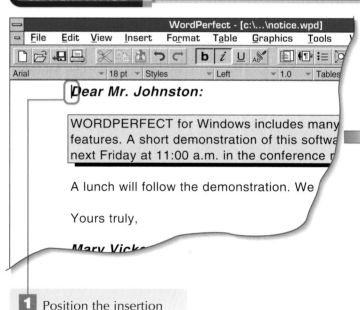

1 Position the insertion point anywhere on the page you want to vertically center.

2 Move the mouse over **Format** and then press the left button.

3 Move the mouse over **Page** and then press the left button.

4 Move the mouse over **Center** and then press the left button.

◆ The **Center Page(s)** dialog box appears.

Format Characters	Format Paragraphs	**Format Pages**	Working With Tables	Using Graphics	Merge Documents	Time Saving Features

- Insert a Page Break
- Change Margins
- **Center a Page**
- Add Page Numbers
- Change Paper Size

- Make Text Fit
- Add Headers or Footers
- Suppress a Header or Footer
- Add Footnotes
- Create Columns

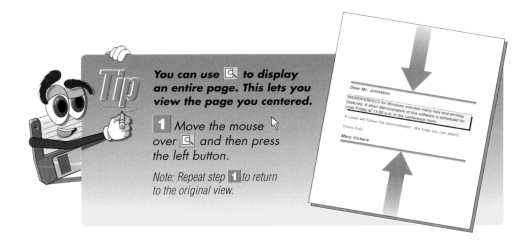

You can use 🔍 to display an entire page. This lets you view the page you centered.

1 Move the mouse over 🔍 and then press the left button.

Note: Repeat step 1 to return to the original view.

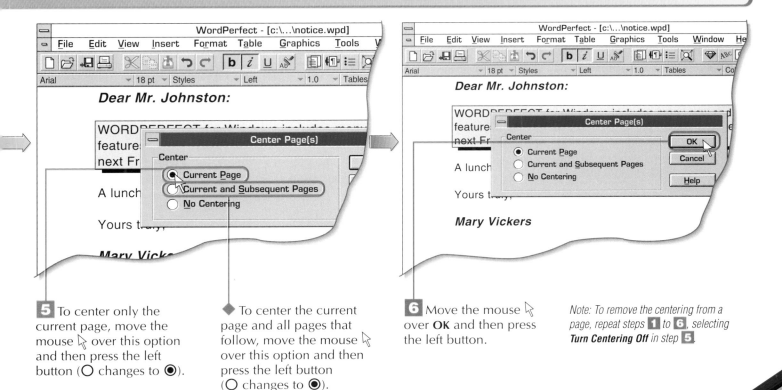

5 To center only the current page, move the mouse over this option and then press the left button (○ changes to ●).

◆ To center the current page and all pages that follow, move the mouse over this option and then press the left button (○ changes to ●).

6 Move the mouse over **OK** and then press the left button.

Note: To remove the centering from a page, repeat steps 1 to 6, selecting Turn Centering Off in step 5.

ADD PAGE NUMBERS

You can have WordPerfect number the pages in your document.

ADD PAGE NUMBERS

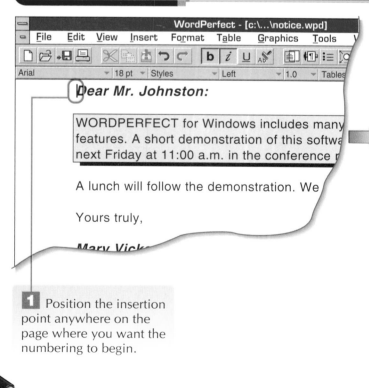

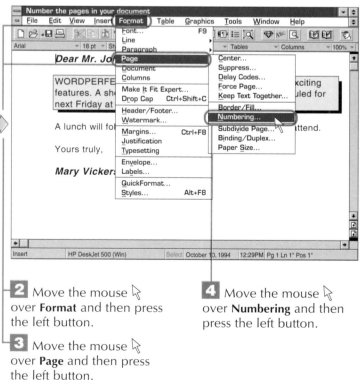

1 Position the insertion point anywhere on the page where you want the numbering to begin.

2 Move the mouse ⌖ over **Format** and then press the left button.

3 Move the mouse ⌖ over **Page** and then press the left button.

4 Move the mouse ⌖ over **Numbering** and then press the left button.

Format Characters	Format Paragraphs	**Format Pages**	Working With Tables	Using Graphics	Merge Documents	Time Saving Features

- Insert a Page Break
- Change Margins
- Center a Page
- **Add Page Numbers**
- Change Paper Size
- Make Text Fit
- Add Headers or Footers
- Suppress a Header or Footer
- Add Footnotes
- Create Columns

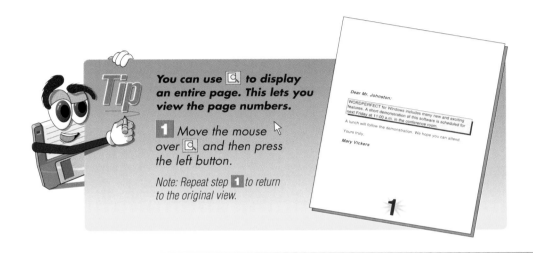

You can use 🔍 to display an entire page. This lets you view the page numbers.

1 Move the mouse over 🔍 and then press the left button.

Note: Repeat step **1** to return to the original view.

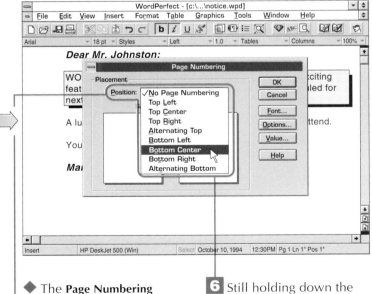

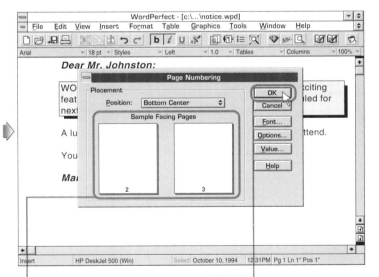

◆ The **Page Numbering** dialog box appears.

5 Move the mouse ⍨ over the box beside **Position:** and then press and hold down the left button.

6 Still holding down the button, move the mouse ⍨ over the position where you want the page numbers to appear (example: **Bottom Center**).

7 Release the button and a sample of the page numbering appears.

8 Move the mouse ⍨ over **OK** and then press the left button.

Note: To remove the page numbers, repeat steps **1** to **8**, selecting **No Page Numbering** in step **6**.

CHANGE PAPER SIZE

> WordPerfect automatically sets each page in your document to print on 8.5 by 11 inch paper. If you want to use a different paper size, you can change this setting.

CHANGE PAPER SIZE

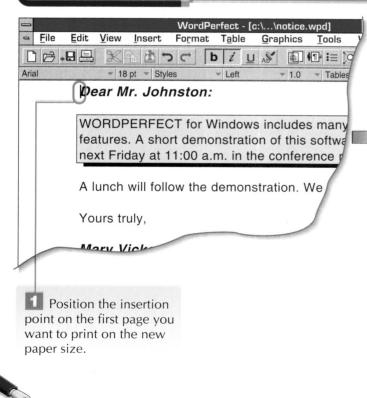

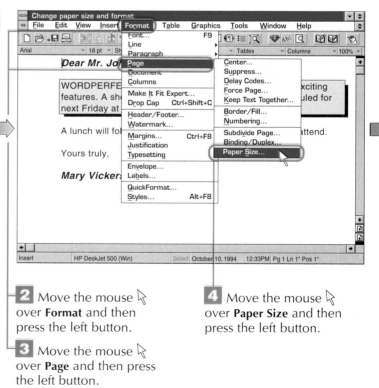

1 Position the insertion point on the first page you want to print on the new paper size.

2 Move the mouse over **Format** and then press the left button.

3 Move the mouse over **Page** and then press the left button.

4 Move the mouse over **Paper Size** and then press the left button.

Format Characters	Format Paragraphs	**Format Pages**	Working With Tables	Using Graphics	Merge Documents	Time Saving Features

- Insert a Page Break
- Change Margins
- Center a Page
- Add Page Numbers
- **Change Paper Size**

- Make Text Fit
- Add Headers or Footers
- Suppress a Header or Footer
- Add Footnotes
- Create Columns

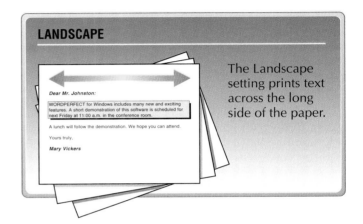

LANDSCAPE

The Landscape setting prints text across the long side of the paper.

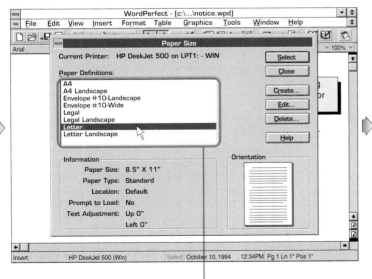

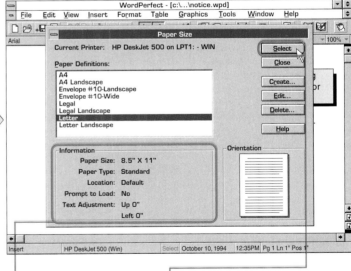

◆ The **Paper Size** dialog box appears.

5 Move the mouse ⇗ over the paper size you want to use and then press the left button.

Note: The available paper sizes depend on the printer you are using.

◆ A description of the paper size you selected appears.

6 Move the mouse ⇗ over **Select** and then press the left button.

◆ The page containing the insertion point and all pages that follow change to the new paper size.

141

MAKE TEXT FIT

You can have WordPerfect shrink or expand your document to fill a specific number of pages.

This feature is useful if the last page in your document contains only a few lines of text and you want it to fit on one less page.

MAKE TEXT FIT

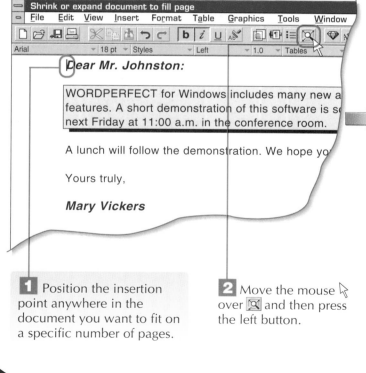

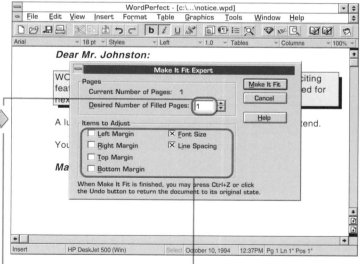

1 Position the insertion point anywhere in the document you want to fit on a specific number of pages.

2 Move the mouse over ☒ and then press the left button.

◆ The **Make It Fit Expert** dialog box appears.

3 Type the number of pages you want your document to fill (example: **1**).

◆ You can have WordPerfect adjust one or more of these items to make your document fit on the number of pages you specified.

Format Characters	Format Paragraphs	**Format Pages**	Working With Tables	Using Graphics	Merge Documents	Time Saving Features

- Insert a Page Break
- Change Margins
- Center a Page
- Add Page Numbers
- Change Paper Size

- **Make Text Fit**
- Add Headers or Footers
- Suppress a Header or Footer
- Add Footnotes
- Create Columns

You can have WordPerfect adjust one or more of the following items to fit text on the number of pages you specify.

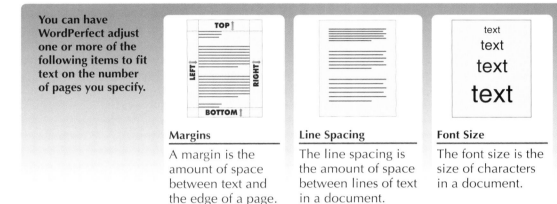

Margins

A margin is the amount of space between text and the edge of a page.

Line Spacing

The line spacing is the amount of space between lines of text in a document.

Font Size

The font size is the size of characters in a document.

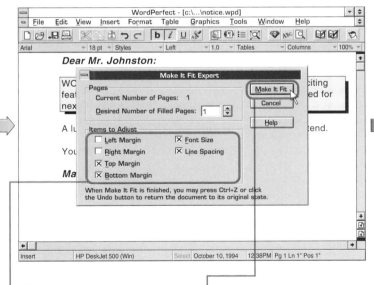

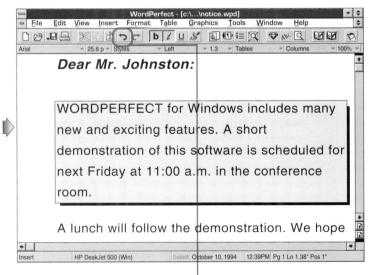

4 To select the item you want WordPerfect to adjust, move the mouse ⊹ over the item and then press the left button (☐ changes to ☒).

5 Repeat step **4** until you have selected all the items you want WordPerfect to adjust.

Note: ☒ *indicates WordPerfect will adjust the item.* ☐ *indicates WordPerfect will **not** adjust the item.*

6 Move the mouse ⊹ over **Make It Fit** and then press the left button.

◆ WordPerfect adjusts the document to fit the number of pages you specified.

◆ To undo the change, move the mouse ⊹ over ↺ and then press the left button.

ADD HEADERS OR FOOTERS

You can add a header or footer to your document to display such information as the date or your company name.

You can print headers and footers on each page or on alternating pages in your document.

Header
A header appears at the top of a page.

Footer
A footer appears at the bottom of a page.

ADD HEADERS OR FOOTERS

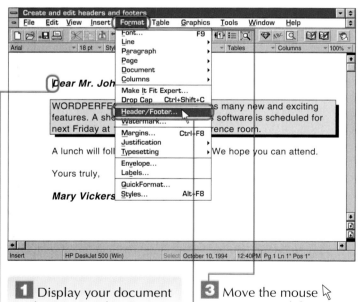

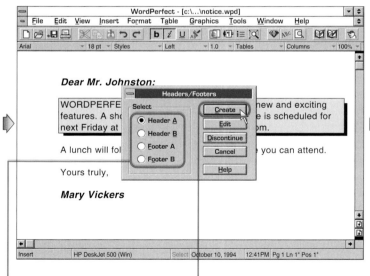

1 Display your document in the Page mode.

2 Position the insertion point at the top of the first page you want to display a header or footer.

3 Move the mouse over **Format** and then press the left button.

4 Move the mouse over **Header/Footer** and then press the left button.

◆ The **Headers/Footers** dialog box appears.

5 Move the mouse over the header or footer you want to create (example: **Header A**) and then press the left button.

*Note: You can create two headers and two footers (**A** and **B**) for each page.*

6 Move the mouse over **Create** and then press the left button.

- Insert a Page Break
- Change Margins
- Center a Page
- Add Page Numbers
- Change Paper Size
- Make Text Fit
- **Add Headers or Footers**
- Suppress a Header or Footer
- Add Footnotes
- Create Columns

DISPLAY AND EDIT HEADERS OR FOOTERS

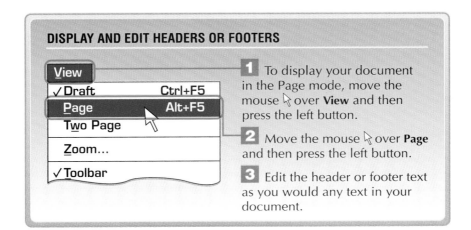

1 To display your document in the Page mode, move the mouse ⍈ over **View** and then press the left button.

2 Move the mouse ⍈ over **Page** and then press the left button.

3 Edit the header or footer text as you would any text in your document.

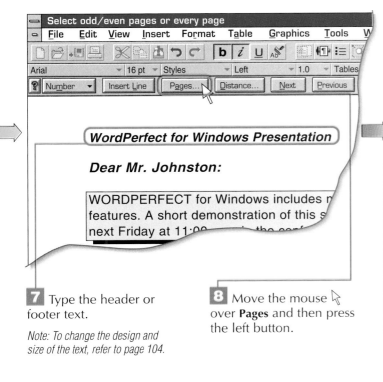

7 Type the header or footer text.

Note: To change the design and size of the text, refer to page 104.

8 Move the mouse ⍈ over **Pages** and then press the left button.

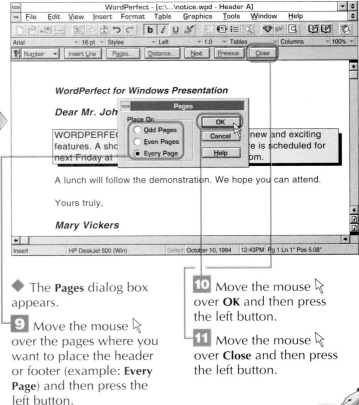

◆ The **Pages** dialog box appears.

9 Move the mouse ⍈ over the pages where you want to place the header or footer (example: **Every Page**) and then press the left button.

10 Move the mouse ⍈ over **OK** and then press the left button.

11 Move the mouse ⍈ over **Close** and then press the left button.

145

SUPPRESS A HEADER OR FOOTER

> If you do not want a header or footer to appear on a page in your document, you can use the Suppress feature to hide the header or footer.

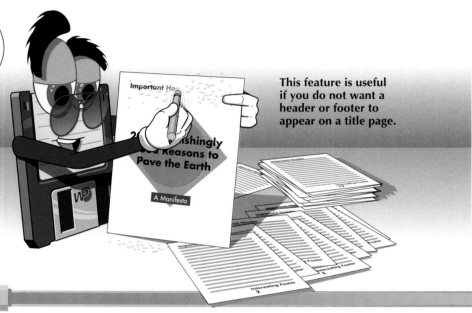

This feature is useful if you do not want a header or footer to appear on a title page.

SUPPRESS A HEADER OR FOOTER

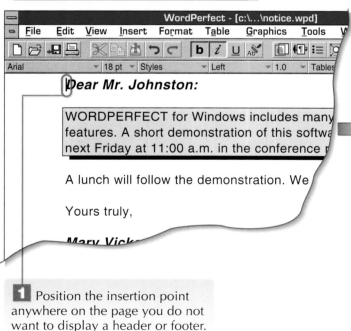

1 Position the insertion point anywhere on the page you do not want to display a header or footer.

2 Move the mouse ↕ over **Format** and then press the left button.

3 Move the mouse ↕ over **Page** and then press the left button.

4 Move the mouse ↕ over **Suppress** and then press the left button.

◆ The **Suppress** dialog box appears.

146

Format Characters	Format Paragraphs	**Format Pages**	Working With Tables	Using Graphics	Merge Documents	Time Saving Features

- Insert a Page Break
- Change Margins
- Center a Page
- Add Page Numbers
- Change Paper Size

- Make Text Fit
- Add Headers or Footers
- **Suppress a Header or Footer**
- Add Footnotes
- Create Columns

Tip

*You can also use the Suppress feature if you do not want a **page number** to appear on a page in your document.*

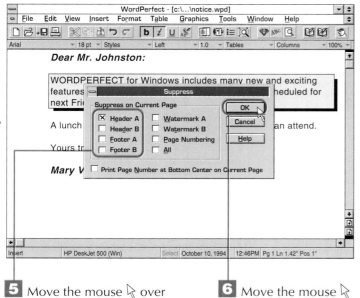

5 Move the mouse � over the header or footer you do not want to appear on the page and then press the left button (☐ changes to ☒).

6 Move the mouse � over **OK** and then press the left button.

DISCONTINUE A HEADER OR FOOTER

You can turn off a header or footer after a certain page in your document. This is useful if you do not want a header or footer to appear on the bibliography pages at the end of a report.

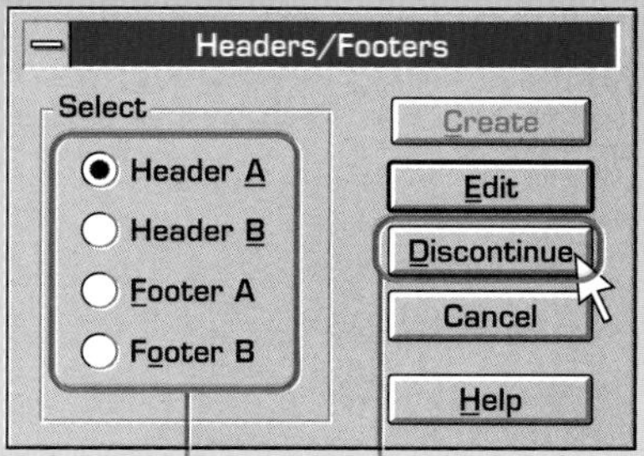

1 Position the insertion point anywhere on the first page you do not want to display a header or footer.

2 Move the mouse � over **Format** and then press the left button.

3 Move the mouse � over **Header/Footer** and then press the left button.

4 Move the mouse � over the header or footer you want to discontinue and then press the left button.

5 Move the mouse � over **Discontinue** and then press the left button.

ADD FOOTNOTES

A footnote appears at the bottom of a page to provide additional information about text in your document.

WordPerfect automatically numbers a footnote and places the footnote on the same page as the text it refers to.

① H. Smith, _Aeronautical Refrigeration Repair_ (California: Quest Publishing, 1989) 10.

② R. Anderson, _Volatile Cold Gases_ (Alaska: Inert Publishing, 1992) 31.

ADD FOOTNOTES

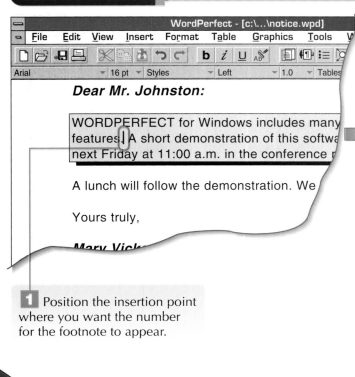

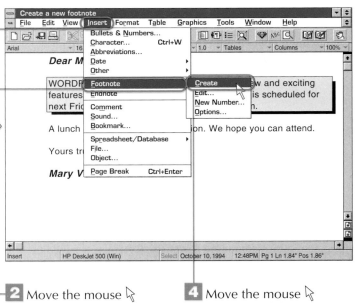

1 Position the insertion point where you want the number for the footnote to appear.

2 Move the mouse ⌖ over **Insert** and then press the left button.

3 Move the mouse ⌖ over **Footnote** and then press the left button.

4 Move the mouse ⌖ over **Create** and then press the left button.

WORKING WITH WORDPERFECT

| Format Characters | Format Paragraphs | **Format Pages** | Working With Tables | Using Graphics | Merge Documents | Time Saving Features |

- Insert a Page Break
- Change Margins
- Center a Page
- Add Page Numbers
- Change Paper Size

- Make Text Fit
- Add Headers or Footers
- Suppress a Header or Footer
- **Add Footnotes**
- Create Columns

DISPLAY AND EDIT FOOTNOTES

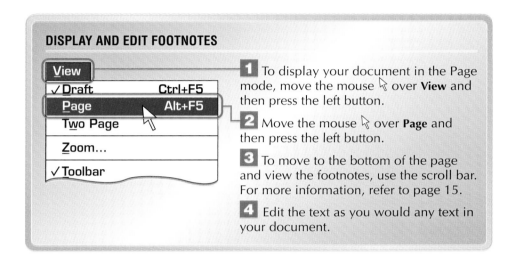

1 To display your document in the Page mode, move the mouse ⬚ over **View** and then press the left button.

2 Move the mouse ⬚ over **Page** and then press the left button.

3 To move to the bottom of the page and view the footnotes, use the scroll bar. For more information, refer to page 15.

4 Edit the text as you would any text in your document.

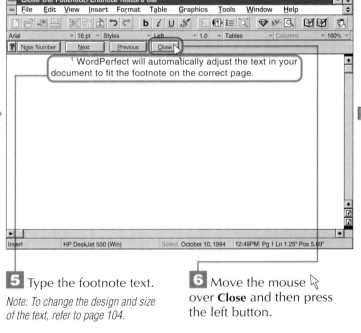

5 Type the footnote text.

Note: To change the design and size of the text, refer to page 104.

6 Move the mouse ⬚ over **Close** and then press the left button.

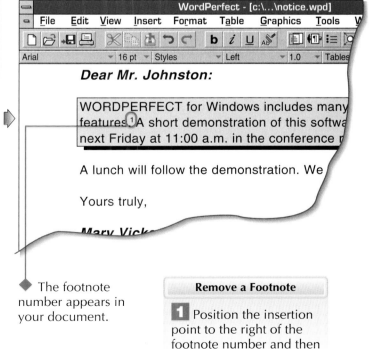

◆ The footnote number appears in your document.

Remove a Footnote

1 Position the insertion point to the right of the footnote number and then press ←Backspace.

149

CREATE COLUMNS

You can display your text in columns like those found in a newspaper. This feature is useful for creating documents such as newsletters and brochures.

CREATE COLUMNS

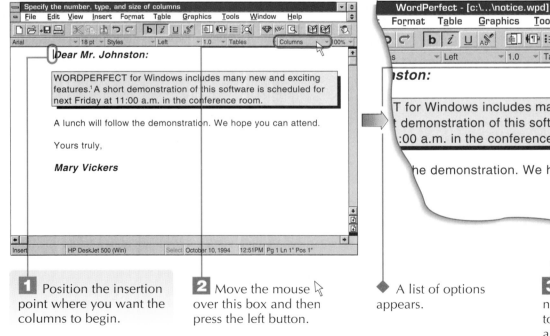

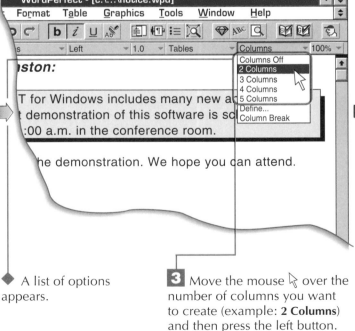

1 Position the insertion point where you want the columns to begin.

2 Move the mouse over this box and then press the left button.

◆ A list of options appears.

3 Move the mouse over the number of columns you want to create (example: **2 Columns**) and then press the left button.

INSERT A COLUMN BREAK

You can insert a column break to move text from the bottom of one column to the top of the next. This is useful when you want to keep all the text in a paragraph together.

Column

Break

1 Position the insertion point to the left of the first character in the paragraph you want to move to the next column.

2 Press Ctrl + Enter on your keyboard.

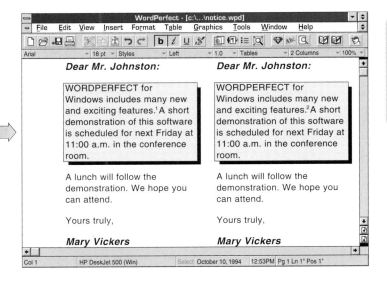

TURN COLUMNS OFF

1 Position the insertion point where you want to turn off the columns.

2 Perform steps **2** and **3**, selecting **Columns Off** in step **3**.

◆ The text following the insertion point appears in columns.

Note: In this example, the existing text was copied to demonstrate the new column format. To copy text, refer to page 34.

verview

WORKING WITH TABLES

In this chapter you will learn how to create a table to organize the information in your document.

CREATE A TABLE

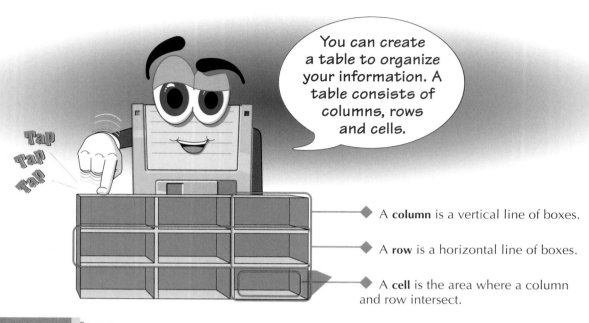

You can create a table to organize your information. A table consists of columns, rows and cells.

◆ A **column** is a vertical line of boxes.

◆ A **row** is a horizontal line of boxes.

◆ A **cell** is the area where a column and row intersect.

CREATE A TABLE

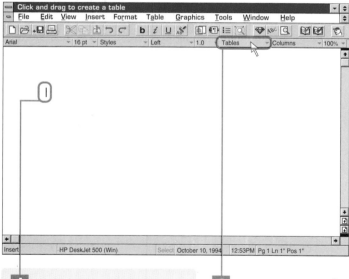

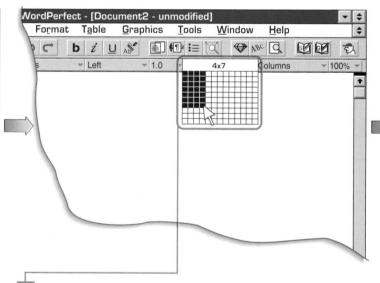

1 Position the insertion point where you want the table to appear in your document.

Note: This example adds a table to a new document. To create a new document, refer to page 90.

2 Move the mouse over this box.

3 Press and hold down the left button as you move the mouse over the table size you want to create (example: **4x7**).

WORKING WITH WORDPERFECT

| Format Characters | Format Paragraphs | Format Pages | **Working With Tables** | Using Graphics | Merge Documents | Time Saving Features |

- **Create a Table**
- Change Column Width
- Select Cells
- Add a Row or Column
- Delete a Row or Column
- Join Cells
- Add Numbers in a Table
- Change Number Type
- Change Table Lines
- Using the Table Expert

MOVE IN A TABLE (Using the Keyboard)

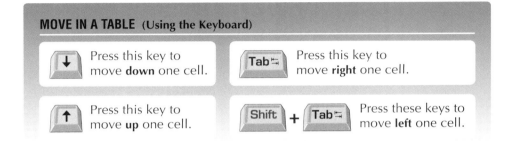

↓ Press this key to move **down** one cell.	Tab ⇆ Press this key to move **right** one cell.
↑ Press this key to move **up** one cell.	Shift + Tab ⇆ Press these keys to move **left** one cell.

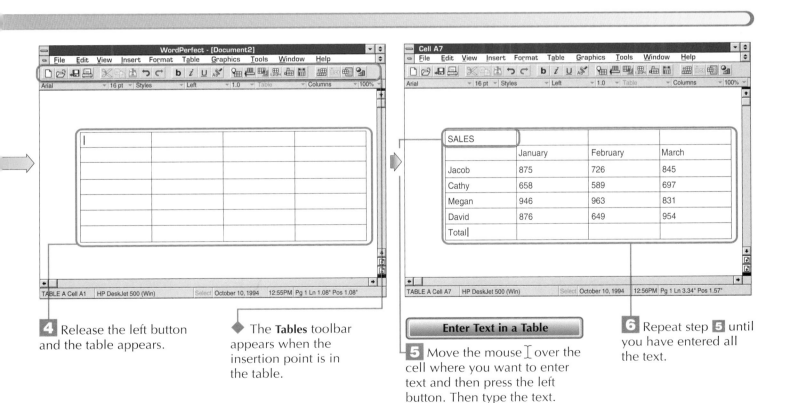

4 Release the left button and the table appears.

◆ The **Tables** toolbar appears when the insertion point is in the table.

Enter Text in a Table

5 Move the mouse I over the cell where you want to enter text and then press the left button. Then type the text.

6 Repeat step **5** until you have entered all the text.

You can change the width of columns to better display the information in your table.

CHANGE COLUMN WIDTH

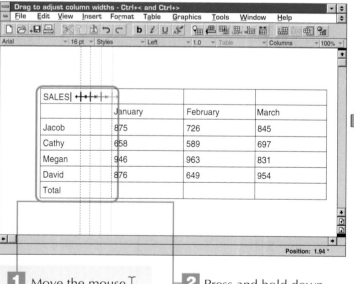

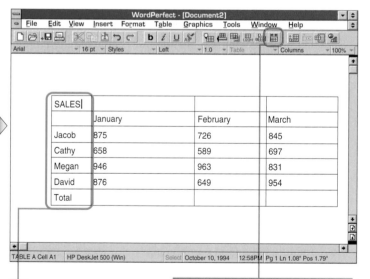

1 Move the mouse I over the left or right edge of the column you want to adjust and I changes to $+$.

2 Press and hold down the left button as you drag the edge of the column to a new position.

◆ A dotted line indicates the new position.

3 Release the button and the new column width appears.

QUICKLY CHANGE COLUMN WIDTH

1 To change the width of a column to fit the longest item, position the insertion point in the column you want to change.

2 Move the mouse � over ▦ and then press the left button.

156

Before you can make changes to your table, you must select the cells you want to modify. Selected cells appear highlighted on your screen.

SELECT CELLS

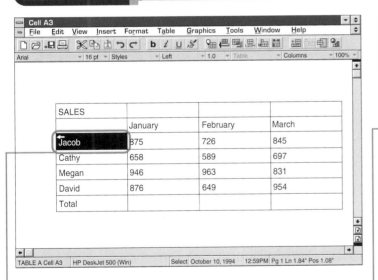

Select a Cell

1 Move the mouse I over the left edge of the cell (I changes to ⇐) and then press the left button.

Note: To deselect cells, move the mouse I outside the selected area and then press the left button.

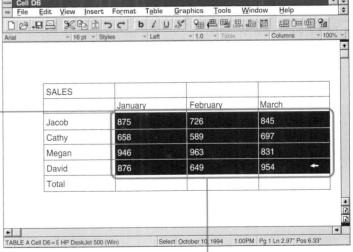

Select Several Cells

1 Move the mouse I over the first cell you want to select and then press and hold down the left button.

2 Still holding down the button, move the mouse ⇐ until you highlight all the cells you want to select. Then release the button.

157

ADD A ROW
OR COLUMN

You can add
a row or column
to your table if you
want to insert new
information.

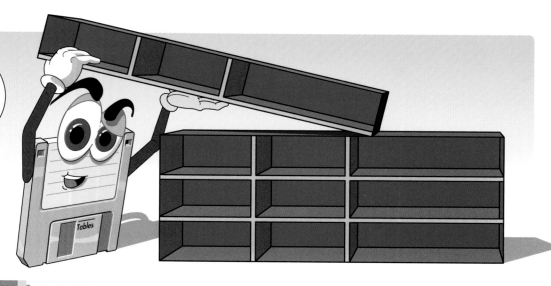

ADD A ROW OR COLUMN

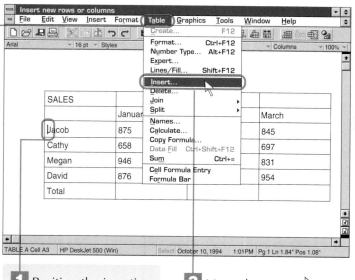

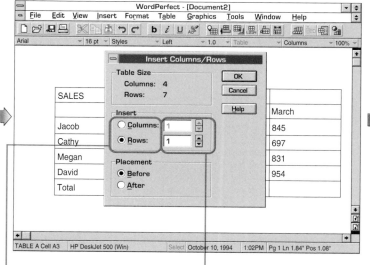

1 Position the insertion point where you want to add a row or column.

2 Move the mouse ⩔ over **Table** and then press the left button.

3 Move the mouse ⩔ over **Insert** and then press the left button.

◆ The **Insert Columns/Rows** dialog box appears.

4 To add a row, move the mouse ⩔ over **Rows:** and then press the left button.

◆ To add a column, move the mouse ⩔ over **Columns:** and then press the left button.

5 Type the number of rows or columns you want to add (example: **1**).

Format Characters	Format Paragraphs	Format Pages	**Working With Tables**	Using Graphics	Merge Documents	Time Saving Features

- Create a Table
- Change Column Width
- Select Cells
- **Add a Row or Column**
- Delete a Row or Column
- Join Cells
- Add Numbers in a Table
- Change Number Type
- Change Table Lines
- Using the Table Expert

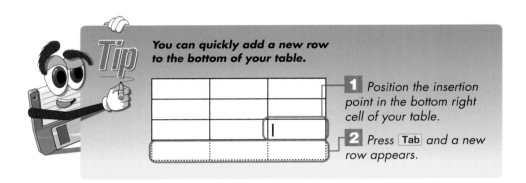

You can quickly add a new row to the bottom of your table.

1 Position the insertion point in the bottom right cell of your table.

2 Press **Tab** and a new row appears.

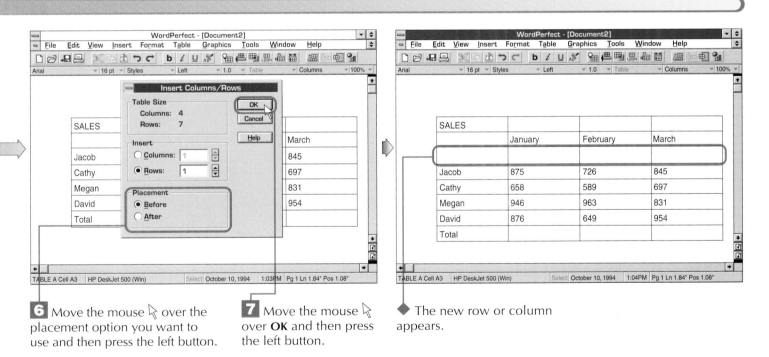

6 Move the mouse ⌖ over the placement option you want to use and then press the left button.

Note: **Before** places the new row or column before the cell containing the insertion point. **After** places the new row or column after the cell containing the insertion point.

7 Move the mouse ⌖ over **OK** and then press the left button.

◆ The new row or column appears.

159

DELETE A ROW OR COLUMN

You can delete a row or column from your table. This lets you remove extra cells you no longer need.

DELETE A ROW OR COLUMN

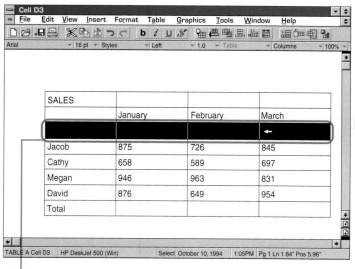

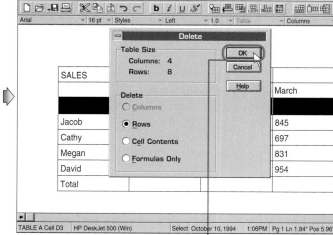

1 Select all the cells in the row or column you want to delete.

Note: To select cells, refer to page 157.

2 Press **Delete** on your keyboard.

◆ The **Delete** dialog box appears.

3 To delete the row or column you selected, move the mouse � over **OK** and then press the left button.

Format Characters	Format Paragraphs	Format Pages	Working With Tables	Using Graphics	Merge Documents	Time Saving Features

Working With Tables

- Create a Table
- Change Column Width
- Select Cells
- Add a Row or Column
- **Delete a Row or Column**
- Join Cells
- Add Numbers in a Table
- Change Number Type
- Change Table Lines
- Using the Table Expert

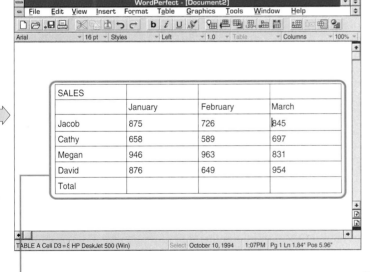

◆ The row or column disappears.

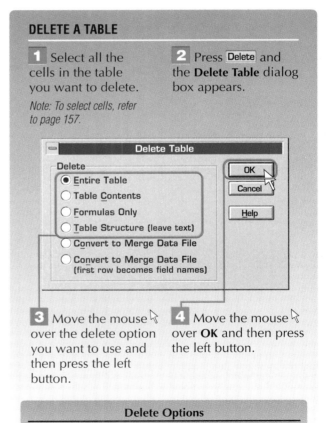

DELETE A TABLE

1 Select all the cells in the table you want to delete.

Note: To select cells, refer to page 157.

2 Press `Delete` and the **Delete Table** dialog box appears.

Delete Table

Delete
- ● Entire Table
- ○ Table Contents
- ○ Formulas Only
- ○ Table Structure (leave text)
- ○ Convert to Merge Data File
- ○ Convert to Merge Data File (first row becomes field names)

OK | Cancel | Help

3 Move the mouse ⬚ over the delete option you want to use and then press the left button.

4 Move the mouse ⬚ over **OK** and then press the left button.

Delete Options

Entire Table	Table Contents	Table Structure
Deletes the text and table lines.	Deletes only the text.	Deletes only the table lines.

JOIN CELLS

You can combine two or more cells in your table to make one large cell. This is useful if you want to display a title across the top of your table.

JOIN CELLS

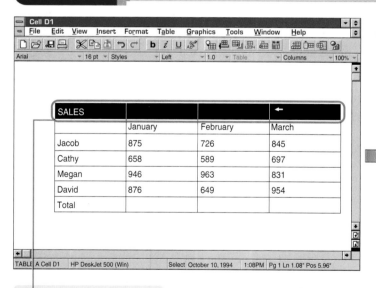

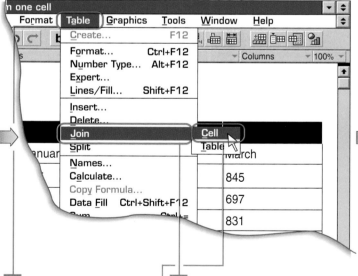

1 Select the cells you want to join.

Note: To select cells, refer to page 157.

2 Move the mouse ᐅ over **Table** and then press the left button.

3 Move the mouse ᐅ over **Join** and then press the left button.

4 Move the mouse ᐅ over **Cell** and then press the left button.

WORKING WITH WORDPERFECT

| Format Characters | Format Paragraphs | Format Pages | **Working With Tables** | Using Graphics | Merge Documents | Time Saving Features |

- Create a Table
- Change Column Width
- Select Cells
- Add a Row or Column
- Delete a Row or Column

- **• Join Cells**
- Add Numbers in a Table
- Change Number Type
- Change Table Lines
- Using the Table Expert

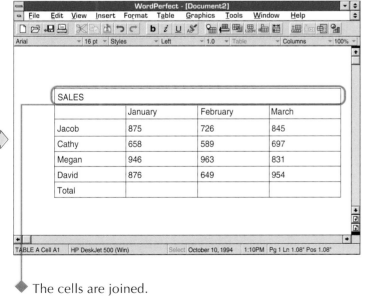

SALES			
	January	February	March
Jacob	875	726	845
Cathy	658	589	697
Megan	946	963	831
David	876	649	954
Total			

◆ The cells are joined.

SPLIT CELLS

You can split one cell into two or more cells.

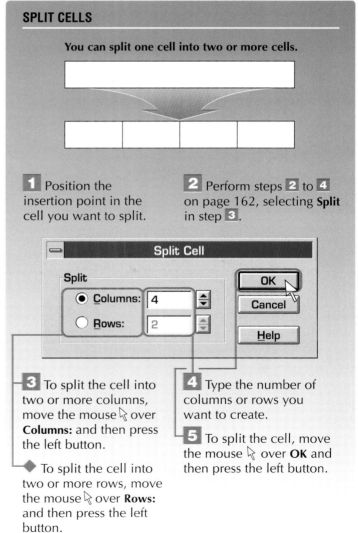

1 Position the insertion point in the cell you want to split.

2 Perform steps **2** to **4** on page 162, selecting **Split** in step **3**.

3 To split the cell into two or more columns, move the mouse ⟍ over **Columns:** and then press the left button.

◆ To split the cell into two or more rows, move the mouse ⟍ over **Rows:** and then press the left button.

4 Type the number of columns or rows you want to create.

5 To split the cell, move the mouse ⟍ over **OK** and then press the left button.

163

ADD NUMBERS IN A TABLE

You can use the Sum feature to quickly add a list of numbers in your table.

ADD NUMBERS IN A TABLE

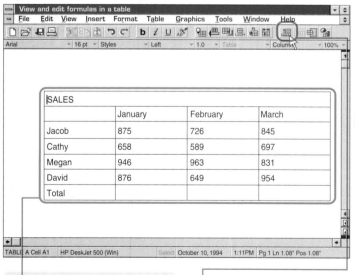

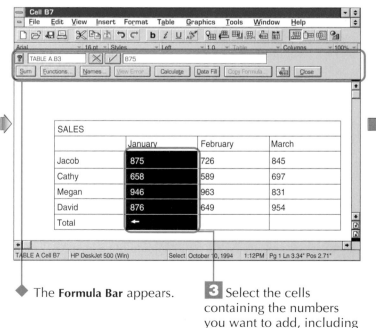

1 Position the insertion point anywhere in the table containing the numbers you want to add.

2 To display the **Formula Bar**, move the mouse ↖ over 🎹 and then press the left button.

◆ The **Formula Bar** appears.

3 Select the cells containing the numbers you want to add, including an empty cell for the result.

Note: To select cells, refer to page 157.

If you change a number in your table, you can use the Calculate feature to update the totals.

Calculate

1 Perform steps **1** and **2** on page 164.

2 Move the mouse ⬠ over **Calculate** on the **Formula Bar** and then press the left button.

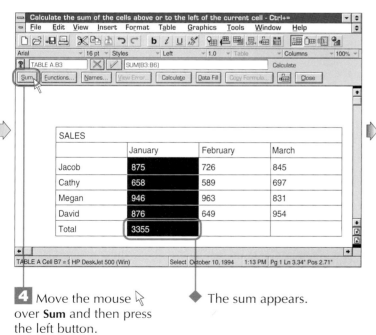

4 Move the mouse ⬠ over **Sum** and then press the left button.

◆ The sum appears.

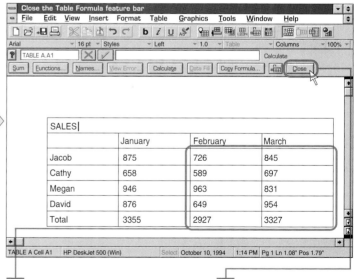

5 Repeat steps **3** and **4** for each list of numbers you want to sum.

Note: To deselect cells, move the mouse ⌶ outside the selected area and then press the left button.

6 To hide the **Formula Bar,** move the mouse ⬠ over **Close** and then press the left button.

CHANGE NUMBER TYPE

You can change the appearance of numbers in your table without having to retype them. This can make the numbers easier to understand.

Commas	1,037.82
Currency	$1,037.82
Date/Time	October 10,1994
Integer	1038
Percent	103782.00%
Scientific	1.04e+03

CHANGE NUMBER TYPE

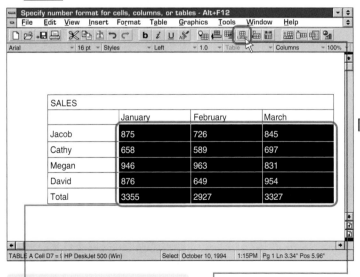

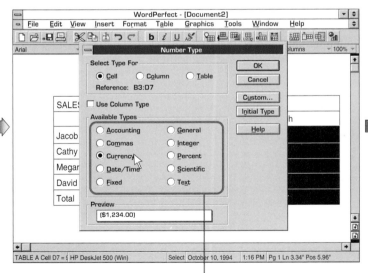

1 Select the cells in the table that contain the numbers you want to change.

Note: To select cells, refer to page 157.

2 Move the mouse over 🔲 and then press the left button.

◆ The **Number Type** dialog box appears.

3 Move the mouse over the number type you want to use and then press the left button (○ changes to ●).

166

| Format Characters | Format Paragraphs | Format Pages | Working With Tables | Using Graphics | Merge Documents | Time Saving Features |

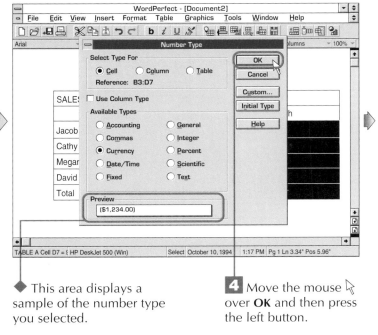

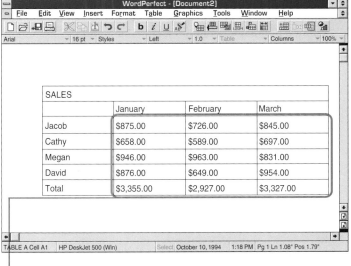

◆ This area displays a sample of the number type you selected.

4 Move the mouse ↖ over **OK** and then press the left button.

◆ The appearance of the numbers changes.

Note: To deselect cells, move the mouse I outside the selected area and then press the left button.

CHANGE TABLE LINES

You can emphasize information and enhance the appearance of your table by changing the table lines. WordPerfect offers several line styles that you can choose from.

CHANGE TABLE LINES

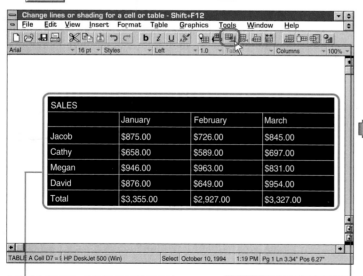

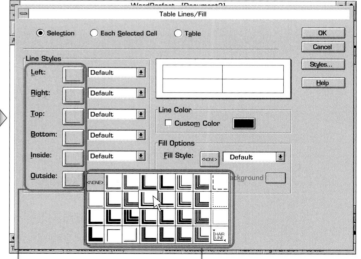

1 Select the cells in the table that contain the lines you want to change.

Note: To select cells, refer to page 157.

2 Move the mouse ▷ over and then press the left button.

3 Move the mouse ▷ over the box beside the line you want to change (example: **Outside**) and then press the left button.

◆ The available line styles appear.

4 Move the mouse ▷ over the line style you want to use and then press the left button.

*Note: Repeat steps **3** and **4** for each line you want to change.*

| Format Characters | Format Paragraphs | Format Pages | Working With Tables | Using Graphics | Merge Documents | Time Saving Features |

- Create a Table
- Change Column Width
- Select Cells
- Add a Row or Column
- Delete a Row or Column
- Join Cells
- Add Numbers in a Table
- Change Number Type
- **Change Table Lines**
- Using the Table Expert

You can format text in a table as you would any text in your document.

1 Select the cells containing the text you want to format.

Note: To select cells, refer to page 157.

2 To change the alignment of text, refer to page 114.

◆ To change the font of text, refer to page 104.

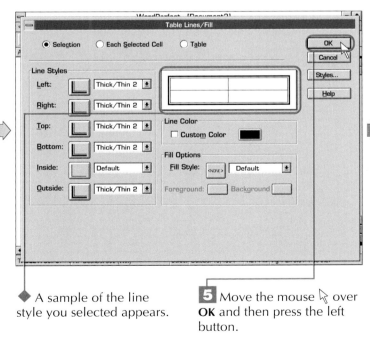

◆ A sample of the line style you selected appears.

5 Move the mouse ⬚ over **OK** and then press the left button.

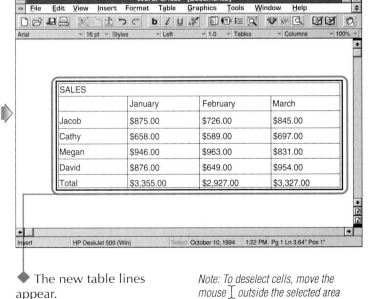

◆ The new table lines appear.

Note: To deselect cells, move the mouse I outside the selected area and then press the left button.

169

USING THE TABLE EXPERT

You can save time by using the Table Expert feature to enhance the appearance of a table. WordPerfect provides forty table designs that you can choose from.

USING THE TABLE EXPERT

Quickly modify a table's appearance, or create and edit table styles

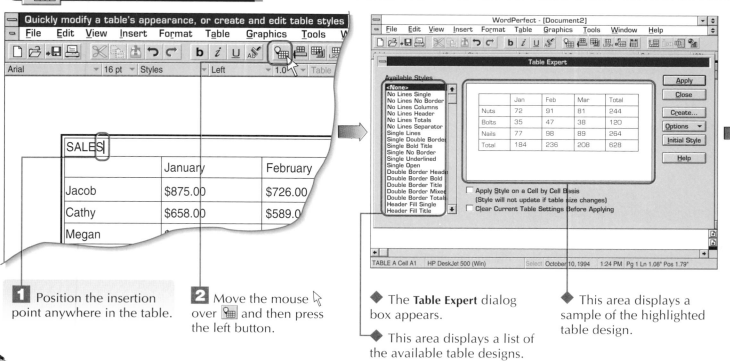

1 Position the insertion point anywhere in the table.

2 Move the mouse over the button and then press the left button.

◆ The **Table Expert** dialog box appears.

◆ This area displays a list of the available table designs.

◆ This area displays a sample of the highlighted table design.

| Format Characters | Format Paragraphs | Format Pages | Working With Tables | Using Graphics | Merge Documents | Time Saving Features |

- Create a Table
- Change Column Width
- Select Cells
- Add a Row or Column
- Delete a Row or Column
- Join Cells
- Add Numbers in a Table
- Change Number Type
- Change Table Lines
- **Using the Table Expert**

To remove a Table Expert design from your table:

Perform steps **1** to **4** below, selecting <**None**> in step **3**.

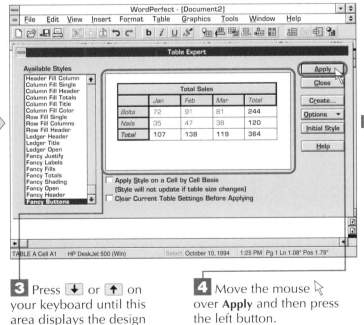

3 Press ↓ or ↑ on your keyboard until this area displays the design you want to use (example: **Fancy Buttons**).

4 Move the mouse over **Apply** and then press the left button.

◆ WordPerfect applies the design you selected to the table.

Overview

USING GRAPHICS

Add an Image

Move an Image

Size an Image

Change Text Wrap

In this chapter you will learn how to use graphics to give your document a more interesting and professional look.

ADD AN IMAGE

You can make your document more interesting by adding an image. WordPerfect provides over eighty images that you can choose from.

ADD AN IMAGE

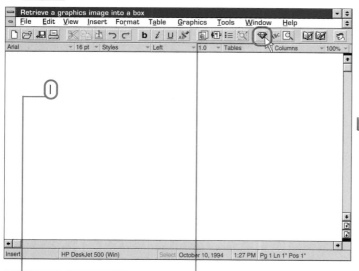

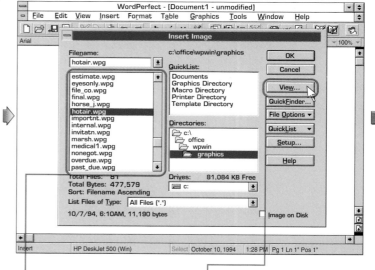

1 Position the insertion point where you want the image to appear.

Note: This example adds an image to a new document. To create a new document, refer to page 90.

2 Move the mouse ⤢ over 💎 and then press the left button.

◆ The **Insert Image** dialog box appears.

3 Move the mouse ⤢ over an image of interest (example: **hotair.wpg**) and then press the left button.

Note: To view all of the available images, use the scroll bar. For more information, refer to page 15.

4 To preview the image, move the mouse ⤢ over **View** and then press the left button.

174

Format Characters	Format Paragraphs	Format Pages	Working With Tables	Using Graphics	Merge Documents	Time Saving Features

Using Graphics
- • **Add an Image**
- • Move an Image
- • Size an Image
- • Change Text Wrap

DELETE AN IMAGE FROM YOUR DOCUMENT

1 To select the image you want to delete, move the mouse ⍫ over the image and then press the left button.

2 Press Delete on your keyboard.

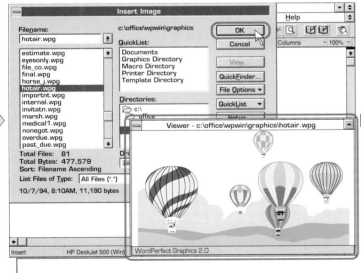

◆ The image appears.

Note: To quickly preview the available images, press ⬇ or ⬆ on your keyboard.

5 To add the displayed image to your document, move the mouse ⍫ over **OK** and then press the left button.

◆ The image appears in your document.

◆ The **Graphics Box** feature bar also appears. You can use this bar to make changes to the image.

6 To remove the feature bar from your screen, move the mouse ⍫ over **Close** and then press the left button.

MOVE AN IMAGE   SIZE AN IMAGE

You can move an image to a more suitable location in your document. You can also change the overall size of an image.

MOVE AN IMAGE

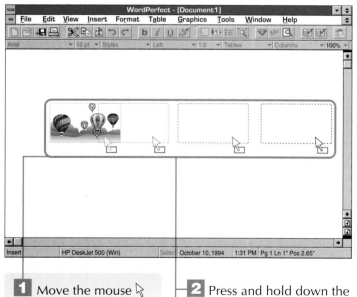

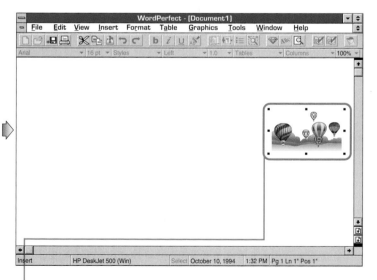

1 Move the mouse ⬚ over the image you want to move.

2 Press and hold down the left button as you drag the image to a new location.

◆ A dotted rectangular box indicates the new location.

3 Release the button and the image appears in the new location.

WORKING WITH WORDPERFECT

| Format Characters | Format Paragraphs | Format Pages | Working With Tables | Using Graphics | Merge Documents | Time Saving Features |

- Add an Image
- **Move an Image**
- **Size an Image**
- Change Text Wrap

You can use any square around an image to change its size.

■ You can use these squares to change the height of an image.

□ You can use these squares to change the width of an image.

■ You can use these squares to change the height and width of an image at the same time.

SIZE AN IMAGE

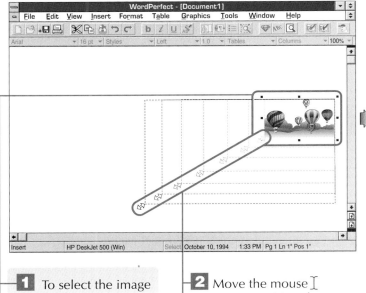

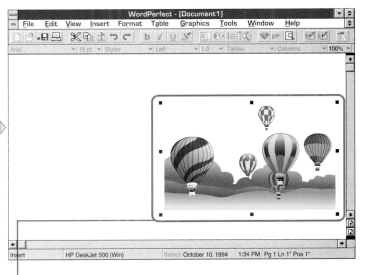

1 To select the image you want to size, move the mouse ⬚ over the image and then press the left button.

◆ Squares (■) appear around the image.

2 Move the mouse I over a square (■) and I changes to ⬚.

3 Press and hold down the left button as you drag the image to the desired size.

4 Release the button and the image changes to the new size.

177

CHANGE TEXT WRAP

You can change the way text flows around an image in your document. This can give your document a more professional look.

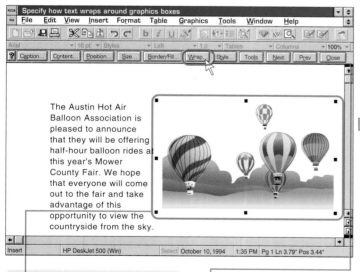

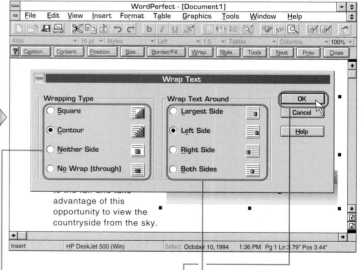

◆ The **Wrap Text** dialog box appears.

1 To change the way text flows around an image, move the mouse Ⓚ over the image and then press the left button.

2 Move the mouse ⓀⓀ over **Wrap** and then press the left button.

*Note: If the **Wrap** button does not appear on your screen, refer to the Tip on page 179.*

3 Move the mouse ⓀⓀ over the type of text wrapping you want to use and then press the left button (○ changes to ◉).

4 Move the mouse ⓀⓀ over the side of the image where you want the text to appear and then press the left button (○ changes to ◉).

5 Move the mouse ⓀⓀ over **OK** and then press the left button.

178

WORKING WITH WORDPERFECT

| Format Characters | Format Paragraphs | Format Pages | Working With Tables | **Using Graphics** | Merge Documents | Time Saving Features |

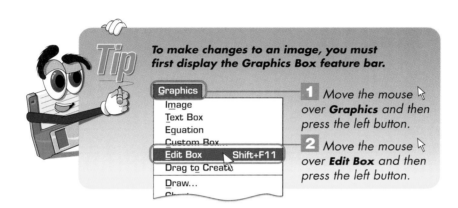

To make changes to an image, you must first display the Graphics Box feature bar.

Graphics
Image
Text Box
Equation
Custom Box...
Edit Box   Shift+F11
Drag to Create
Draw...

1 *Move the mouse over **Graphics** and then press the left button.*

2 *Move the mouse over **Edit Box** and then press the left button.*

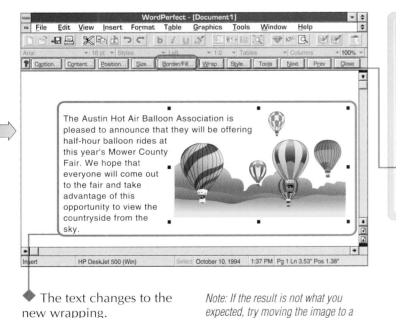

◆ The text changes to the new wrapping.

Note: If the result is not what you expected, try moving the image to a new location. For more information, refer to page 176.

ADD BORDERS AND SHADING

You can easily add borders and shading to an image.

1 Move the mouse over the image you want to display borders and shading and then press the left button.

2 Move the mouse over **Border/Fill** and then press the left button.

*Note: If the **Border/Fill** button does not appear on your screen, refer to the Tip above.*

3 To select border and shading styles, refer to page 126.

verview

MERGE DOCUMENTS

Introduction

Create a Data File

Create a Form File

Merge Files

Using Merge to Print Envelopes

◆ In this chapter you will learn how to produce personalized letters and envelopes for each person on your mailing list.

INTRODUCTION

You can use the Merge feature to produce personalized letters for each person on your mailing list. To do this, you must first create a form file and a data file.

FORM FILE

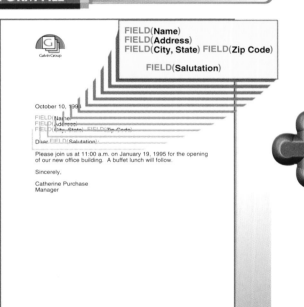

A form file contains the text that will appear in each letter. It also contains FIELD codes that tell WordPerfect where to insert the personalized information that changes in each letter.

DATA FILE

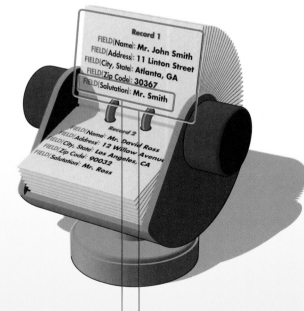

A data file contains the information for each person you want to send the letter to (example: names and addresses).

◆ The information for each person is called a **record**.

◆ The information within each record is broken down into **fields**.

Format Characters	Format Paragraphs	Format Pages	Working With Tables	Using Graphics	Merge Documents	Time Saving Features

- **Introduction**
- Create a Data File
- Create a Form File
- Merge Files
- Using Merge to Print Envelopes

MERGED FILE

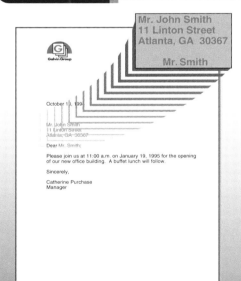

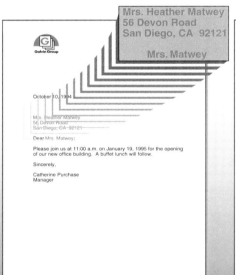

When you merge the files, WordPerfect inserts the personalized information from the data file into the form file.

CREATE A DATA FILE

A data file contains the information for each person you want to send a letter to. This file may include information such as names and addresses.

Record 1
FIELD(Name): Mr. John Smith
FIELD(Address): 11 Linton Street
FIELD(City, State): Atlanta, GA
FIELD(Zip Code): 30367
FIELD(Salutation): Mr. Smith

CREATE A DATA FILE

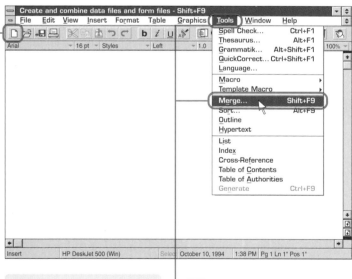

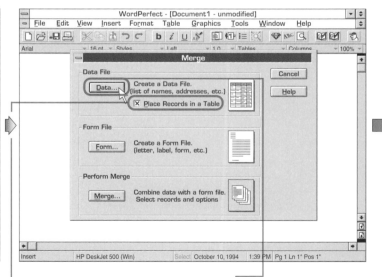

1 To create a new document, move the mouse ⌖ over 🗅 and then press the left button.

2 To create a data file, move the mouse ⌖ over **Tools** and then press the left button.

3 Move the mouse ⌖ over **Merge** and then press the left button.

◆ The **Merge** dialog box appears.

4 To place your information in a table, move the mouse ⌖ over this option and then press the left button (☐ changes to ☒).

5 Move the mouse ⌖ over **Data** and then press the left button.

184

| Format Characters | Format Paragraphs | Format Pages | Working With Tables | Using Graphics | Merge Documents | Time Saving Features |

- Introduction
- **Create a Data File**
- Create a Form File
- Merge Files
- Using Merge to Print Envelopes

FIELD NAMES

A **field name** is a label that you give to each category of information in your data file.

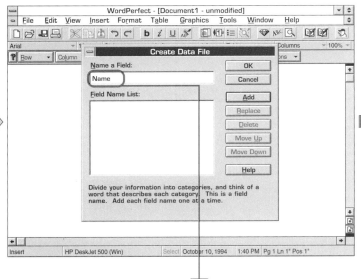

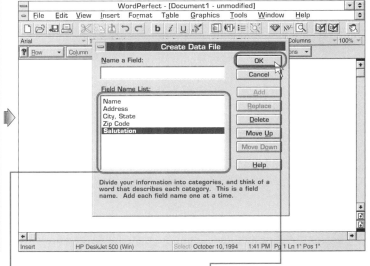

◆ The **Create Data File** dialog box appears.

6 Type a name for the first field (example: **Name**) and then press **Enter**.

7 Repeat step **6** for each field name you want to add.

◆ This area displays the field names you entered.

8 When you finish entering all the field names, move the mouse ⬉ over **OK** and then press the left button.

To continue, refer to the next page.

You only have to create a data file once. You can use the information from the data file with any future letter you create.

CREATE A DATA FILE (CONTINUED)

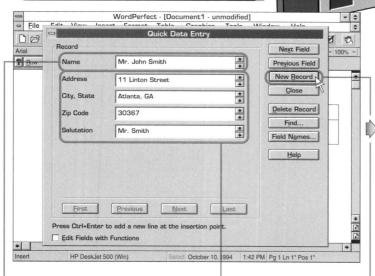

◆ The **Quick Data Entry** dialog box appears displaying blank areas where you can enter the information for one customer.

9 Type the information that corresponds to the first field (example: **Mr. John Smith**). Press **Tab** to move to the next field.

10 Repeat step **9** until you finish typing all the information for the customer.

11 To add information for a new customer, move the mouse ↕ over **New Record** and then press the left button.

12 Repeat steps **9** to **11** for each customer.

13 When you finish entering the information for each customer on your mailing list, move the mouse ↕ over **Close** and then press the left button.

WORKING WITH WORDPERFECT

| Format Characters | Format Paragraphs | Format Pages | Working With Tables | Using Graphics | **Merge Documents** | Time Saving Features |

• Introduction
• **Create a Data File**
• Create a Form File
• Merge Files
• Using Merge to Print Envelopes

If a customer's mailing address changes, you can edit the information displayed in the table.

Note: To edit text, refer to pages 24 to 26.

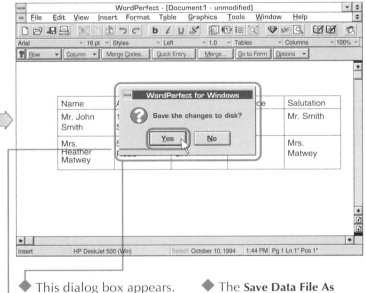

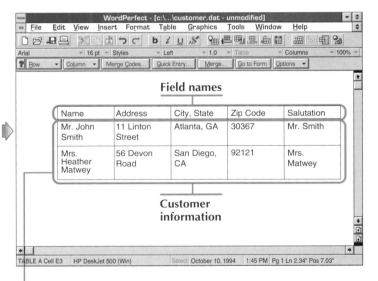

◆ This dialog box appears.

14 To save the document, move the mouse ⬚ over **Yes** and then press the left button.

◆ The **Save Data File As** dialog box appears.

15 Type a name for your data file (example: **customer**) and then press **Enter**.

Note: For more information on saving a document, refer to page 56.

◆ The information you entered appears in a table.

◆ Each row in the table displays information for one customer.

CREATE A FORM FILE

A form file contains the text that will appear in each letter. It also contains codes that tell WordPerfect where to insert the information from the data file.

CREATE A FORM FILE

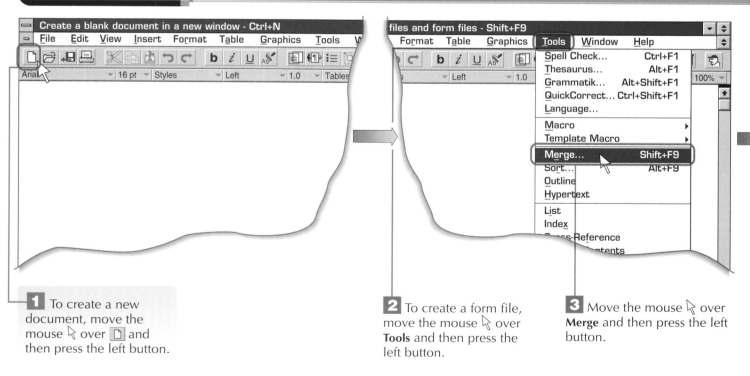

1 To create a new document, move the mouse ⟨ over ⟐ and then press the left button.

2 To create a form file, move the mouse ⟨ over **Tools** and then press the left button.

3 Move the mouse ⟨ over **Merge** and then press the left button.

Format Characters	Format Paragraphs	Format Pages	Working With Tables	Using Graphics	**Merge Documents**	Time Saving Features

- Introduction
- Create a Data File
- **Create a Form File**
- Merge Files
- Using Merge to Print Envelopes

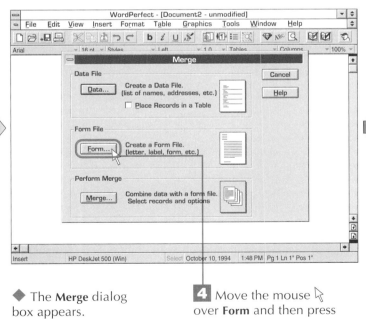

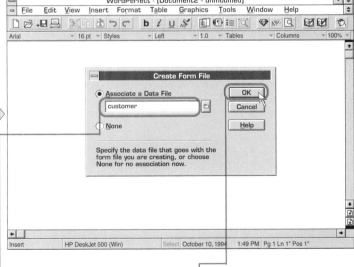

◆ The **Merge** dialog box appears.

4 Move the mouse ⍄ over **Form** and then press the left button.

◆ The **Create Form File** dialog box appears.

5 Type the name of the data file that contains the information you want to place in the letter (example: **customer**).

6 Move the mouse ⍄ over **OK** and then press the left button.

To continue, refer to the next page.

CREATE A FORM FILE

When you merge the data and form files, the information from the data file will replace the codes you inserted in the letter.

CREATE A FORM FILE (CONTINUED)

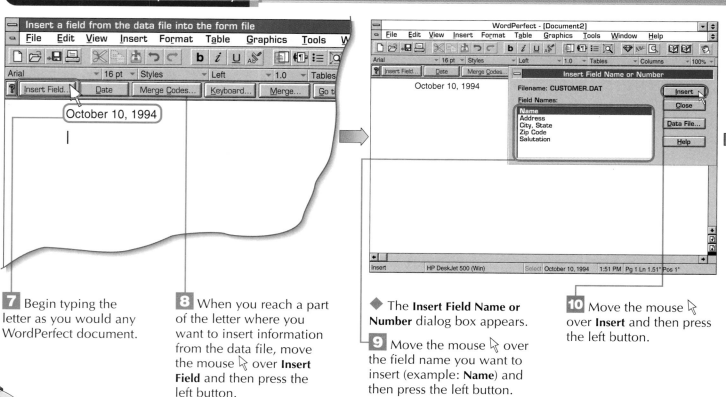

7 Begin typing the letter as you would any WordPerfect document.

8 When you reach a part of the letter where you want to insert information from the data file, move the mouse � over **Insert Field** and then press the left button.

◆ The **Insert Field Name or Number** dialog box appears.

9 Move the mouse � over the field name you want to insert (example: **Name**) and then press the left button.

10 Move the mouse � over **Insert** and then press the left button.

190

Format Characters	Format Paragraphs	Format Pages	Working With Tables	Using Graphics	**Merge Documents**	Time Saving Features

- Introduction
- Create a Data File
- • **Create a Form File**
- Merge Files
- Using Merge to Print Envelopes

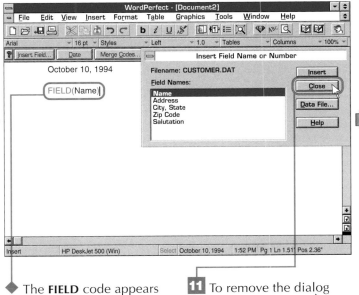

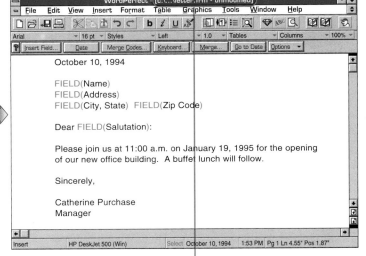

◆ The **FIELD** code appears in your document.

Note: To insert the next field name on the following line, press **Enter** *. To insert the next field name on the same line, press the* **Spacebar**.

11 To remove the dialog box, move the mouse ⟍ over **Close** and then press the left button.

12 Continue typing the letter, repeating steps **8** to **11** for each field name you want to insert.

13 When you finish typing the letter, save the document. In this example, the document is named **letter**.

Note: To save a document, refer to page 56.

MERGE FILES

The Merge feature combines a form file and a data file to create a personalized letter for each person on your mailing list.

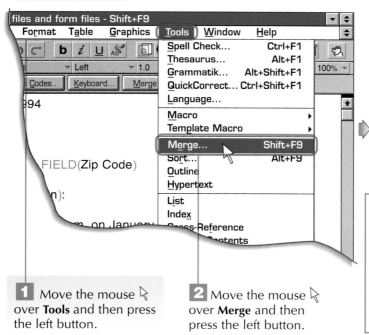

1 Move the mouse ⌖ over **Tools** and then press the left button.

2 Move the mouse ⌖ over **Merge** and then press the left button.

◆ The **Merge** dialog box appears.

3 Move the mouse ⌖ over **Merge** and then press the left button.

◆ The **Perform Merge** dialog box appears.

| Format Characters | Format Paragraphs | Format Pages | Working With Tables | Using Graphics | Merge Documents | Time Saving Features |

◆ *To conserve hard disk space, do not save the merged document after printing. You can easily recreate this document by repeating steps 1 to 5 below.*

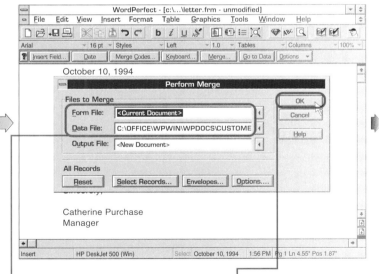

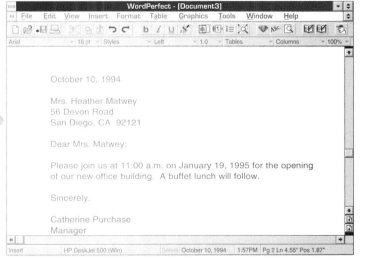

◆ WordPerfect displays the names of the files it will merge.

4 If the correct names of the files you want to merge are not displayed, press **Tab** until you highlight the filename you want to change. Type the correct name.

5 Move the mouse ⇖ over **OK** and then press the left button.

◆ The form and data files are merged.

6 To view the letters, use the scroll bar.

Note: For more information on using the scroll bar, refer to page 15.

◆ You can edit and print this document as you would any WordPerfect document.

193

USING MERGE TO PRINT ENVELOPES

You can use the Merge feature to print an envelope for each person on your mailing list.

USING MERGE TO PRINT ENVELOPES

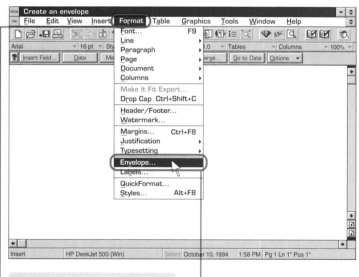

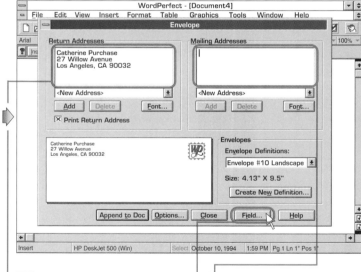

1 Perform steps **1** to **6** starting on page 188.

2 Move the mouse ⌖ over **Format** and then press the left button.

3 Move the mouse ⌖ over **Envelope** and then press the left button.

◆ The **Envelope** dialog box appears.

4 To enter a return address, move the mouse I over this box and then press the left button.

5 Press **+Backspace** or **Delete** to remove any existing text. Then type the return address.

6 To enter the mailing address, move the mouse I over this box and then press the left button.

7 Move the mouse ⌖ over **Field** and then press the left button.

194

Format Characters	Format Paragraphs	Format Pages	Working With Tables	Using Graphics	Merge Documents	Time Saving Features

- Introduction
- Create a Data File
- Create a Form File
- Merge Files
- **Using Merge to Print Envelopes**

IMPORTANT!

To create an envelope for each customer, you must merge the file below with a data file (example: **customer**). To merge files, refer to page 192.

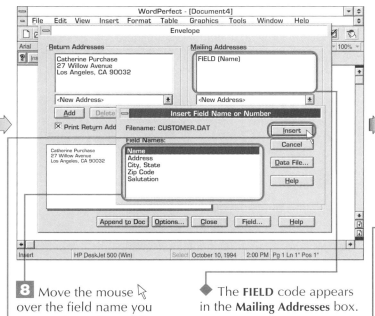

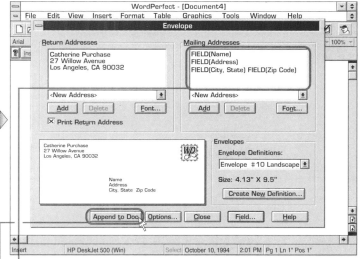

8 Move the mouse ⊾ over the field name you want to insert (example: **Name**) and then press the left button.

9 Move the mouse ⊾ over **Insert** and then press the left button.

◆ The **FIELD** code appears in the **Mailing Addresses** box.

10 To insert the next field name on the following line, press **Enter**.

*Note: To insert the next field name on the same line, press the **Spacebar**.*

11 Repeat steps **7** to **10** for each field name you want to insert.

12 To add the envelope to the current document, move the mouse ⊾ over **Append to Doc** and then press the left button.

13 Save the document.

Note: To save a document, refer to page 56.

195

verview

TIME SAVING FEATURES

Insert the Date

Using a Template

Record a Macro

Play a Macro

In this chapter you will learn how to use special features offered by WordPerfect to help you work more efficiently.

INSERT THE DATE

INSERT THE DATE AS TEXT

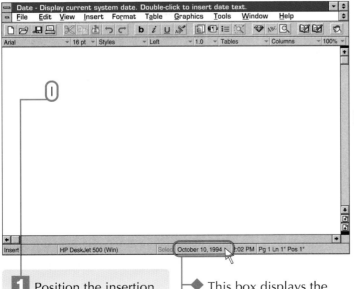

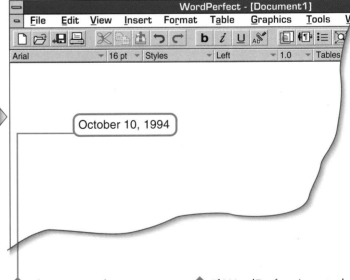

1 Position the insertion point where you want the date to appear.

◆ This box displays the current date.

2 To insert the date into your document, move the mouse ⬡ over this box and then quickly press the left button twice.

◆ The current date appears in your document.

◆ The date will not change unless you retype the text.

◆ If WordPerfect inserts the wrong date in your document, you must change the date set in your computer.

Note: For information on changing the date set in your computer, refer to your Windows manual.

| Format Characters | Format Paragraphs | Format Pages | Working With Tables | Using Graphics | Merge Documents | **Time Saving Features** |

- **Insert the Date**
- Using a Template
- Record a Macro
- Play a Macro

WordPerfect offers two ways to insert the current date into your document.

AS TEXT

If you insert the current date as text, the date will not change unless you retype the text. This is useful when you want a document to always display a particular date.

AS A CODE

If you insert the current date as a code, WordPerfect will automatically update the date every time you open or print the document. This is useful when you want a document to always display the current date.

INSERT THE DATE AS A CODE

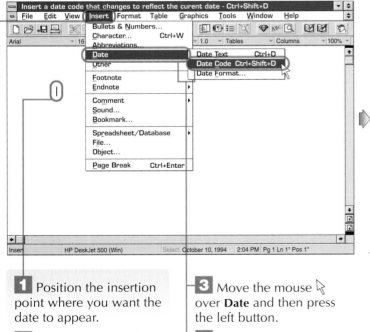

1 Position the insertion point where you want the date to appear.

2 Move the mouse over **Insert** and then press the left button.

3 Move the mouse over **Date** and then press the left button.

4 Move the mouse over **Date Code** and then press the left button.

◆ The current date appears in your document.

◆ WordPerfect will automatically update this date every time you open or print the document.

◆ If WordPerfect inserts the wrong date in your document, you must change the date set in your computer.

Note: For information on changing the date set in your computer, refer to your Windows manual.

USING A TEMPLATE

Templates save you time by providing the basic framework for many commonly used documents.

USING A TEMPLATE

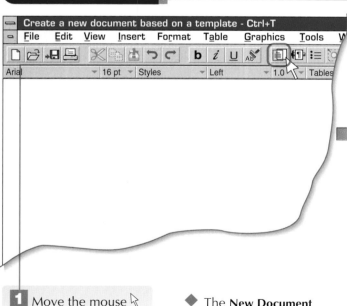

1 Move the mouse ⭦ over 📋 and then press the left button.

◆ The **New Document** dialog box appears.

2 Move the mouse ⭦ over the type of document you want to create and then press the left button.

Note: To view all of the available document types, use the scroll bar. For more information, refer to page 15.

| Format Characters | Format Paragraphs | Format Pages | Working With Tables | Using Graphics | Merge Documents | **Time Saving Features** |

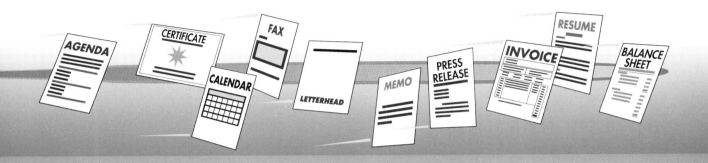

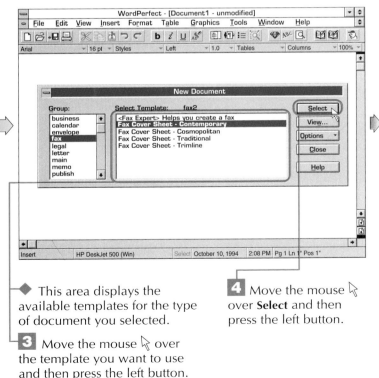

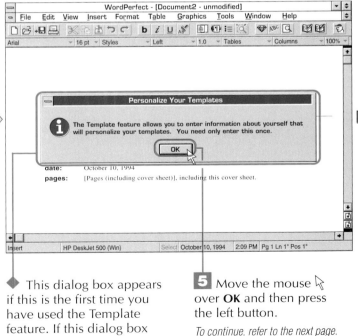

◆ This area displays the available templates for the type of document you selected.

3 Move the mouse �️ over the template you want to use and then press the left button.

4 Move the mouse �️ over **Select** and then press the left button.

◆ This dialog box appears if this is the first time you have used the Template feature. If this dialog box does not appear, skip to step **9** on page 203.

5 Move the mouse �️ over **OK** and then press the left button.

To continue, refer to the next page.

201

USING A TEMPLATE

> The WordPerfect templates complete all the formatting so you can concentrate on the content of your document.

USING A TEMPLATE (CONTINUED)

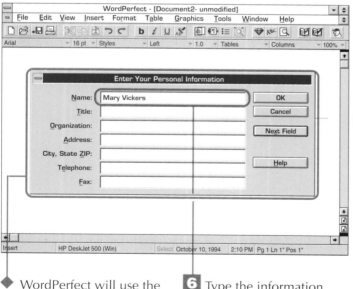

◆ WordPerfect will use the information you enter in this dialog box in all of your templates.

6 Type the information that corresponds to the first category. Then press **Tab** to move to the next category.

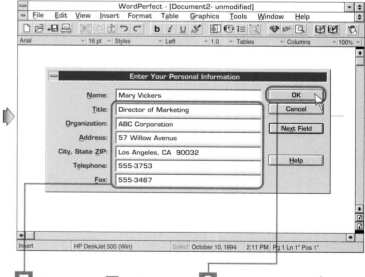

7 Repeat step **6** until you have entered all the required information.

8 Move the mouse ⤷ over **OK** and then press the left button.

Format Characters	Format Paragraphs	Format Pages	Working With Tables	Using Graphics	Merge Documents	**Time Saving Features**

- Insert the Date
- **Using a Template**
- Record a Macro
- Play a Macro

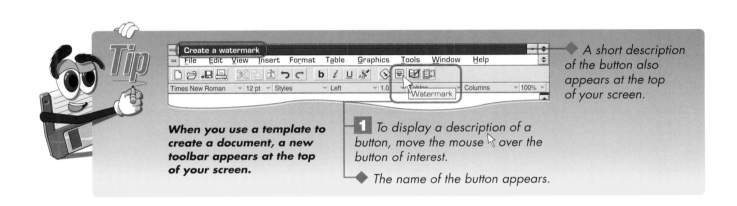

When you use a template to create a document, a new toolbar appears at the top of your screen.

◆ A short description of the button also appears at the top of your screen.

1 To display a description of a button, move the mouse ⩗ over the button of interest.

◆ The name of the button appears.

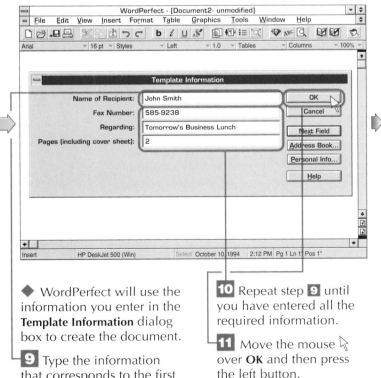

◆ WordPerfect will use the information you enter in the **Template Information** dialog box to create the document.

9 Type the information that corresponds to the first category. Then press **Tab** to move to the next category.

10 Repeat step **9** until you have entered all the required information.

11 Move the mouse ⩗ over **OK** and then press the left button.

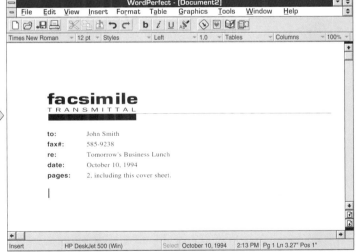

◆ The document appears on your screen.

◆ You can edit and print the document as you would any WordPerfect document.

Note: To view the entire document, use the scroll bar. For more information, refer to page 15.

RECORD A MACRO

A macro saves you time by combining a series of commands into a single command.

RECORD A MACRO

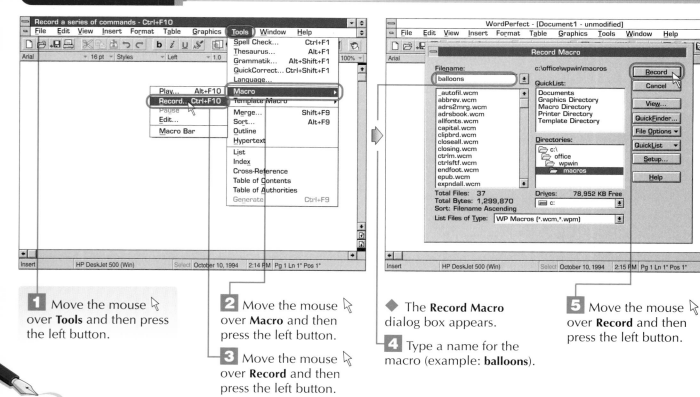

1 Move the mouse ⌖ over **Tools** and then press the left button.

2 Move the mouse ⌖ over **Macro** and then press the left button.

3 Move the mouse ⌖ over **Record** and then press the left button.

◆ The **Record Macro** dialog box appears.

4 Type a name for the macro (example: **balloons**).

5 Move the mouse ⌖ over **Record** and then press the left button.

Format Characters	Format Paragraphs	Format Pages	Working With Tables	Using Graphics	Merge Documents	**Time Saving Features**

- Insert the Date
- Using a Template
- **Record a Macro**
- Play a Macro

IMPORTANT!

While recording a macro, you cannot use the mouse I to move the insertion point or select text.

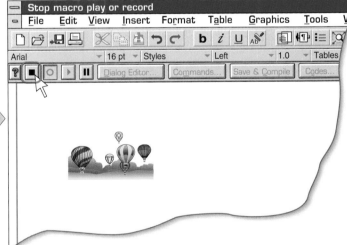

6 Perform the actions you want the macro to record.

Note: In this example, the hot air balloon graphic is inserted into the document. To do so, perform steps 1 to 6 on page 174.

7 When you complete all the actions you want the macro to record, move the mouse ⬚ over ■ and then press the left button.

Note: You can also repeat steps 1 to 3 to stop recording the macro.

205

PLAY A MACRO

When you play a macro, WordPerfect automatically performs the series of commands you assigned to the macro.

PLAY A MACRO

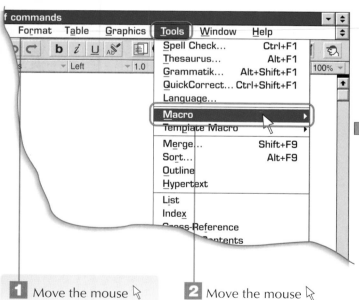

1 Move the mouse ⃗ over **Tools** and then press the left button.

2 Move the mouse ⃗ over **Macro** and then press the left button.

3 Move the mouse ⃗ over **Play** and then press the left button.

◆ The **Play Macro** dialog box appears.

Note: To quickly display the **Play Macro** dialog box, press and hold down **Alt** and then press **F10** on your keyboard.

206

WORKING WITH WORDPERFECT

| Format Characters | Format Paragraphs | Format Pages | Working With Tables | Using Graphics | Merge Documents | **Time Saving Features** |

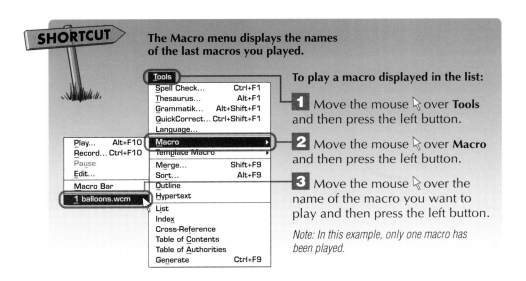

SHORTCUT

The Macro menu displays the names of the last macros you played.

Tools

Spell Check...	Ctrl+F1
Thesaurus...	Alt+F1
Grammatik...	Alt+Shift+F1
QuickCorrect...	Ctrl+Shift+F1
Language...	

Play...	Alt+F10	Macro	▶
Record...	Ctrl+F10	Template Macro	▶
Pause		Merge...	Shift+F9
Edit...		Sort...	Alt+F9
Macro Bar		Outline	
1 balloons.wcm		Hypertext	
		List	
		Index	
		Cross-Reference	
		Table of Contents	
		Table of Authorities	
		Generate	Ctrl+F9

To play a macro displayed in the list:

1 Move the mouse over **Tools** and then press the left button.

2 Move the mouse over **Macro** and then press the left button.

3 Move the mouse over the name of the macro you want to play and then press the left button.

Note: In this example, only one macro has been played.

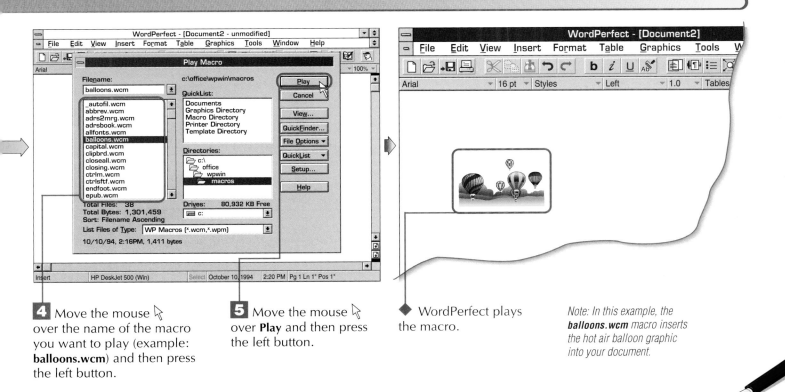

4 Move the mouse over the name of the macro you want to play (example: **balloons.wcm**) and then press the left button.

5 Move the mouse over **Play** and then press the left button.

◆ WordPerfect plays the macro.

*Note: In this example, the **balloons.wcm** macro inserts the hot air balloon graphic into your document.*

207

INDEX

The fun & easy way to learn about computers and more!

Windows 3.1 For Dummies™, 2nd Edition
by Andy Rathbone

ISBN: 1-56884-182-5
$16.95 USA/$22.95 Canada

MORE Windows For Dummies™
by Andy Rathbone

ISBN: 1-56884-048-9
$19.95 USA/$26.95 Canada

DOS For Dummies,® 2nd Edition
by Dan Gookin

ISBN: 1-878058-75-4
$16.95 USA/$22.95 Canada

The Internet For Dummies™
by John Levine & Carol Baroudi

ISBN: 1-56884-024-1
$19.95 USA/$26.95 Canada

Personal Finance For Dummies™
by Eric Tyson

ISBN: 1-56884-150-7
$16.95 USA/$22.95 Canada

PCs For Dummies™, 2nd Edition
by Dan Gookin & Andy Rathbone

ISBN: 1-56884-078-0
$16.95 USA/$22.95 Canada

Macs For Dummies™, 2nd Edition
by David Pogue

ISBN: 1-56884-051-9
$19.95 USA/$26.95 Canada

Over 12 Million in print!

Here's a complete listing of IDG's...*For Dummies* Titles

Title	Author	ISBN #	Price
DATABASE			
Access 2 For Dummies™	by Scott Palmer	ISBN: 1-56884-090-X	$19.95 USA/$26.95 Canada
Access Programming For Dummies™	by Rob Krumm	ISBN: 1-56884-091-8	$19.95 USA/$26.95 Canada
Approach 3 For Windows For Dummies™	by Doug Lowe	ISBN: 1-56884-233-3	$19.99 USA/$26.99 Canada
dBASE For DOS For Dummies™	by Scott Palmer & Michael Stabler	ISBN: 1-56884-188-4	$19.95 USA/$26.95 Canada
dBASE For Windows For Dummies™	by Scott Palmer	ISBN: 1-56884-179-5	$19.95 USA/$26.95 Canada
dBASE 5 For Windows Programming For Dummies™	by Ted Coombs & Jason Coombs	ISBN: 1-56884-215-5	$19.99 USA/$26.99 Canada
FoxPro 2.6 For Windows For Dummies™	by John Kaufeld	ISBN: 1-56884-187-6	$19.95 USA/$26.95 Canada
Paradox 5 For Windows For Dummies™	by John Kaufeld	ISBN: 1-56884-185-X	$19.95 USA/$26.95 Canada
DESKTOP PUBLISHING/ILLUSTRATION/GRAPHICS			
CorelDRAW! 5 For Dummies™	by Deke McClelland	ISBN: 1-56884-157-4	$19.95 USA/$26.95 Canada
CorelDRAW! For Dummies™	by Deke McClelland	ISBN: 1-56884-042-X	$19.95 USA/$26.95 Canada
Harvard Graphics 2 For Windows For Dummies™	by Roger C. Parker	ISBN: 1-56884-092-6	$19.95 USA/$26.95 Canada
PageMaker 5 For Macs For Dummies™	by Galen Gruman & Deke McClelland	ISBN: 1-56884-178-7	$19.95 USA/$26.95 Canada
PageMaker 5 For Windows For Dummies™	by Deke McClelland & Galen Gruman	ISBN: 1-56884-160-4	$19.95 USA/$26.95 Canada
QuarkXPress 3.3 For Dummies™	by Galen Gruman & Barbara Assadi	ISBN: 1-56884-217-1	$19.99 USA/$26.99 Canada
FINANCE/PERSONAL FINANCE/TEST TAKING REFERENCE			
QuickBooks "X" For Dummies™	by Stephen L. Nelson	ISBN: 1-56884-227-9	$19.99 USA/$26.99 Canada
Quicken "X" For DOS For Dummies™, 2nd Edition	by Stephen L. Nelson	ISBN: 1-56884-210-4	$19.95 USA/$26.95 Canada
Quicken "X" For Macs For Dummies™	by Stephen L. Nelson	ISBN: 1-56884-211-2	$19.95 USA/$26.95 Canada
Quicken "X" For Windows For Dummies™, 2nd Edition	by Stephen L. Nelson	ISBN: 1-56884-209-0	$19.95 USA/$26.95 Canada
The SAT I For Dummies™	by Suzee Vlk	ISBN: 1-56884-213-9	$14.99 USA/$20.99 Canada
TurboTax For Windows For Dummies™	by Gail A. Perry, CPA	ISBN: 1-56884-228-7	$19.99 USA/$26.99 Canada
GROUPWARE/INTEGRATED			
Lotus Notes 3.0/3.1 For Dummies™	by Paul Freeland & Stephen Londergan	ISBN: 1-56884-212-0	$19.95 USA/$26.95 Canada
Microsoft Office 4 For Windows For Dummies™	by Roger C. Parker	ISBN: 1-56884-183-3	$19.95 USA/$26.95 Canada
Microsoft Works For Windows 3 For Dummies™	by David C. Kay	ISBN: 1-56884-214-7	$19.99 USA/$26.99 Canada

FOR MORE INFO OR TO ORDER, PLEASE CALL ▶ 800.762.2974 For volume discounts & special orders please call Tony Real, Special Sales, at 415. 312. 0644

Title	Author	ISBN #	Price
INTERNET/COMMUNICATIONS/NETWORKING			
CompuServe For Dummies™	by Wallace Wang	ISBN: 1-56884-181-7	$19.95 USA/$26.95 Canada
Modems For Dummies™, 2nd Edition	by Tina Rathbone	ISBN: 1-56884-223-6	$19.99 USA/$26.99 Canada
Modems For Dummies™	by Tina Rathbone	ISBN: 1-56884-001-2	$19.95 USA/$26.95 Canada
MORE Internet For Dummies™	by John Levine & Margaret Levine Young	ISBN: 1-56884-164-7	$19.95 USA/$26.95 Canada
NetWare For Dummies™	by Ed Tittel & Deni Connor	ISBN: 1-56884-003-9	$19.95 USA/$26.95 Canada
Networking For Dummies™	by Doug Lowe	ISBN: 1-56884-079-9	$19.95 USA/$26.95 Canada
ProComm Plus 2 For Windows For Dummies™	by Wallace Wang	ISBN: 1-56884-219-8	$19.99 USA/$26.95 Canada
The Internet Help Desk For Dummies™	by John Kaufeld	ISBN: 1-56884-238-4	$16.99 USA/$22.99 Canada
The3 Internet For Dummies™, 2nd Edition	by John Levine & Carol Baroudi	ISBN: 1-56884-222-8	$19.99 USA/$26.99 Canada
The Internet For Macs For Dummies™	by Charles Seiter	ISBN: 1-56884-184-1	$19.95 USA/$26.95 Canada
MACINTOSH			
Mac Programming For Dummies™	by Dan Parks Sydow	ISBN: 1-56884-173-6	$19.95 USA/$26.95 Canada
Macintosh System 7.5 For Dummies™	by Bob LeVitus	ISBN: 1-56884-197-3	$19.95 USA/$26.95 Canada
MORE Macs For Dummies™	by David Pogue	ISBN: 1-56884-087-X	$19.95 USA/$26.95 Canada
PageMaker 5 For Macs For Dummies™	by Galen Gruman & Deke McClelland	ISBN: 1-56884-178-7	$19.95 USA/$26.95 Canada
QuarkXPress 3.3 For Dummies™	by Galen Gruman & Barbara Assadi	ISBN: 1-56884-217-1	$19.99 USA/$26.99 Canada
Upgrading and Fixing Macs For Dummies™	by Kearney Rietmann & Frank Higgins	ISBN: 1-56884-189-2	$19.95 USA/$26.95 Canada
MULTIMEDIA			
Multimedia & CD-ROMs For Dummies™, Interactive Multimedia Value Pack	by Andy Rathbone	ISBN: 1-56884-225-2	$29.95 USA/$39.95 Canada
Multimedia & CD-ROMs For Dummies™	by Andy Rathbone	ISBN: 1-56884-089-6	$19.95 USA/$26.95 Canada
OPERATING SYSTEMS/DOS			
MORE DOS For Dummies™	by Dan Gookin	ISBN: 1-56884-046-2	$19.95 USA/$26.95 Canada
S.O.S. For DOS™	by Katherine Murray	ISBN: 1-56884-043-8	$12.95 USA/$16.95 Canada
OS/2 For Dummies™	by Andy Rathbone	ISBN: 1-878058-76-2	$19.95 USA/$26.95 Canada
UNIX			
UNIX For Dummies™	by John Levine & Margaret Levine Young	ISBN: 1-878058-58-4	$19.95 USA/$26.95 Canada
WINDOWS			
S.O.S. For Windows™	by Katherine Murray	ISBN: 1-56884-045-4	$12.95 USA/$16.95 Canada
Windows "X" For Dummies™, 3rd Edition	by Andy Rathbone	ISBN: 1-56884-240-6	$19.99 USA/$26.99 Canada
PCS/HARDWARE			
Illustrated Computer Dictionary For Dummies™	by Dan Gookin, Wally Wang, & Chris Van Buren	ISBN: 1-56884-004-7	$12.95 USA/$16.95 Canada
Upgrading and Fixing PCs For Dummies™	by Andy Rathbone	ISBN: 1-56884-002-0	$19.95 USA/$26.95 Canada
PRESENTATION/AUTOCAD			
AutoCAD For Dummies™	by Bud Smith	ISBN: 1-56884-191-4	$19.95 USA/$26.95 Canada
PowerPoint 4 For Windows For Dummies™	by Doug Lowe	ISBN: 1-56884-161-2	$16.95 USA/$22.95 Canada
PROGRAMMING			
Borland C++ For Dummies™	by Michael Hyman	ISBN: 1-56884-162-0	$19.95 USA/$26.95 Canada
"Borland's New Language Product" For Dummies™	by Neil Rubenking	ISBN: 1-56884-200-7	$19.95 USA/$26.95 Canada
C For Dummies™	by Dan Gookin	ISBN: 1-878058-78-9	$19.95 USA/$26.95 Canada
C++ For Dummies™	by S. Randy Davis	ISBN: 1-56884-163-9	$19.95 USA/$26.95 Canada
Mac Programming For Dummies™	by Dan Parks Sydow	ISBN: 1-56884-173-6	$19.95 USA/$26.95 Canada
QBasic Programming For Dummies™	by Douglas Hergert	ISBN: 1-56884-093-4	$19.95 USA/$26.95 Canada
Visual Basic "X" For Dummies™, 2nd Edition	by Wallace Wang	ISBN: 1-56884-230-9	$19.99 USA/$26.99 Canada
Visual Basic 3 For Dummies™	by Wallace Wang	ISBN: 1-56884-076-4	$19.95 USA/$26.95 Canada
SPREADSHEET			
1-2-3 For Dummies™	by Greg Harvey	ISBN: 1-878058-60-6	$16.95 USA/$22.95 Canada
1-2-3 For Windows 5 For Dummies™, 2nd Edition	by John Walkenbach	ISBN: 1-56884-216-3	$16.95 USA/$22.95 Canada
1-2-3 For Windows For Dummies™	by John Walkenbach	ISBN: 1-56884-052-7	$16.95 USA/$22.95 Canada
Excel 5 For Macs For Dummies™	by Greg Harvey	ISBN: 1-56884-186-8	$19.95 USA/$26.95 Canada
Excel For Dummies™, 2nd Edition	by Greg Harvey	ISBN: 1-56884-050-0	$16.95 USA/$22.95 Canada
MORE Excel 5 For Windows For Dummies™	by Greg Harvey	ISBN: 1-56884-207-4	$19.95 USA/$26.95 Canada
Quattro Pro 6 For Windows For Dummies™	by John Walkenbach	ISBN: 1-56884-174-4	$19.95 USA/$26.95 Canada
Quattro Pro For DOS For Dummies™	by John Walkenbach	ISBN: 1-56884-023-3	$16.95 USA/$22.95 Canada
UTILITIES			
Norton Utilities 8 For Dummies™	by Beth Slick	ISBN: 1-56884-166-3	$19.95 USA/$26.95 Canada
VCRS/CAMCORDERS			
VCRs & Camcorders For Dummies™	by Andy Rathbone & Gordon McComb	ISBN: 1-56884-229-5	$14.99 USA/$20.99 Canada
WORD PROCESSING			
Ami Pro For Dummies™	by Jim Meade	ISBN: 1-56884-049-7	$19.95 USA/$26.95 Canada
More Word For Windows 6 For Dummies™	by Doug Lowe	ISBN: 1-56884-165-5	$19.95 USA/$26.95 Canada
MORE WordPerfect 6 For Windows For Dummies™	by Margaret Levine Young & David C. Kay	ISBN: 1-56884-206-6	$19.95 USA/$26.95 Canada
MORE WordPerfect 6 For DOS For Dummies™	by Wallace Wang, edited by Dan Gookin	ISBN: 1-56884-047-0	$19.95 USA/$26.95 Canada
S.O.S. For WordPerfect™	by Katherine Murray	ISBN: 1-56884-053-5	$12.95 USA/$16.95 Canada
Word 6 For Macs For Dummies™	by Dan Gookin	ISBN: 1-56884-190-6	$19.95 USA/$26.95 Canada
Word For Windows 6 For Dummies™	by Dan Gookin	ISBN: 1-56884-075-6	$16.95 USA/$22.95 Canada
Word For Windows 2 For Dummies™	by Dan Gookin	ISBN: 1-878058-86-X	$16.95 USA/$22.95 Canada
WordPerfect 6 For Dummies™	by Dan Gookin	ISBN: 1-878058-77-0	$16.95 USA/$22.95 Canada
WordPerfect For Dummies™	by Dan Gookin	ISBN: 1-878058-52-5	$16.95 USA/$22.95 Canada
WordPerfect For Windows For Dummies™	by Margaret Levine Young & David C. Kay	ISBN: 1-56884-032-2	$16.95 USA/$22.95 Canada

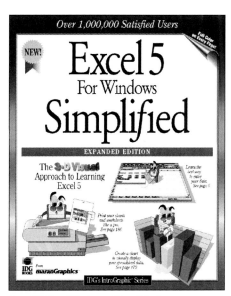
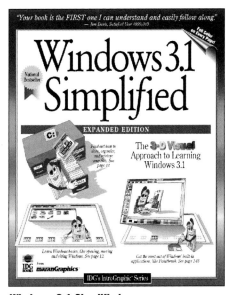

IDG BOOKS

TRADE & INDIVIDUAL ORDERS

Phone: **(800) 762-2974** *or* **(317) 895-5200**
(8 a.m.–6 p.m., CST, weekdays)
FAX : **(317) 895-5298**

CORPORATE ORDERS FOR 3-D VISUAL™ SERIES

Phone: **(800) 469-6616** *ext.* **206**
(8 a.m.–5 p.m., EST, weekdays)
FAX : **(905) 890-9434**

Qty	ISBN	Title	Price	Total

Shipping & Handling Charges

	Description	First book	Each add'l. book	Total
Domestic	Normal	$4.50	$1.50	$
	Two Day Air	$8.50	$2.50	$
	Overnight	$18.00	$3.00	$
International	Surface	$8.00	$8.00	$
	Airmail	$16.00	$16.00	$
	DHL Air	$17.00	$17.00	$

Subtotal _____

CA residents add applicable sales tax _____

IN, MA and MD residents add 5% sales tax _____

IL residents add 6.25% sales tax _____

RI residents add 7% sales tax _____

TX residents add 8.25% sales tax _____

Shipping _____

Total _____

Ship to:

Name_____

Address_____

Company_____

City/State/Zip_____

Daytime Phone_____

Payment: ☐ Check to IDG Books (US Funds Only)

☐ Visa ☐ Mastercard ☐ American Express

Card # _____ Exp. _____ Signature_____

IDG Books Education Group
Jim Kelly, Director of Education Sales – 9 Village Circle, Ste. 450, Westlake, TX 76262
800-434-2086 Phone • 817-430-5852 Fax • 8:30-5:00 CST

IDG BOOKS WORLDWIDE REGISTRATION CARD

Title of this book: WordPerfect 6.1 For Windows Simplified

My overall rating of this book: ❑ Very good [1] ❑ Good [2] ❑ Satisfactory [3] ❑ Fair [4] ❑ Poor [5]

How I first heard about this book:

❑ Found in bookstore; name: [6] _____   ❑ Book review: [7] _____

❑ Advertisement: [8] _____   ❑ Catalog: [9] _____

❑ Word of mouth; heard about book from friend, co-worker, etc.: [10]   ❑ Other: [11] _____

What I liked most about this book:

_____
_____
_____

What I would change, add, delete, etc., in future editions of this book:

_____
_____
_____

Other comments:

_____
_____

Number of computer books I purchase in a year: ❑ 1 [12] ❑ 2-5 [13] ❑ 6-10 [14] ❑ More than 10 [15]

I would characterize my computer skills as: ❑ Beginner [16] ❑ Intermediate [17] ❑ Advanced [18] ❑ Professional [19]

I use ❑ DOS [20] ❑ Windows [21] ❑ OS/2 [22] ❑ Unix [23] ❑ Macintosh [24] ❑ Other: [25] _____

(please specify)

I would be interested in new books on the following subjects:
(please check all that apply, and use the spaces provided to identify specific software)

❑ Word processing: [26] _____   ❑ Spreadsheets: [27] _____

❑ Data bases: [28] _____   ❑ Desktop publishing: [29] _____

❑ File Utilities: [30] _____   ❑ Money management: [31] _____

❑ Networking: [32] _____   ❑ Programming languages: [33] _____

❑ Other: [34] _____

I use a PC at (please check all that apply): ❑ home [35] ❑ work [36] ❑ school [37] ❑ other: [38] _____

The disks I prefer to use are ❑ 5.25 [39] ❑ 3.5 [40] ❑ other: [41] _____

I have a CD ROM: ❑ yes [42] ❑ no [43]

I plan to buy or upgrade computer hardware this year: ❑ yes [44] ❑ no [45]

I plan to buy or upgrade computer software this year: ❑ yes [46] ❑ no [47]

Name: _____   Business title: [48] _____   Type of Business: [49] _____

Address (❑ home [50] ❑ work [51]/Company name: _____)

Street/Suite# _____

City [52]/State [53]/Zipcode [54]: _____   Country [55] _____

❑ **I liked this book!** You may quote me by name in future
IDG Books Worldwide promotional materials.

My daytime phone number is _____

IDG BOOKS

®

THE WORLD OF COMPUTER KNOWLEDGE

❏ **YES!**

Please keep me informed about IDG's World of Computer Knowledge.
Send me the latest IDG Books catalog.